W9-BLG-902

2859

LC
501
.M217   McCluskey
          Catholic education
          in America, a
          documentary history

Date Due

AU 14 '73			

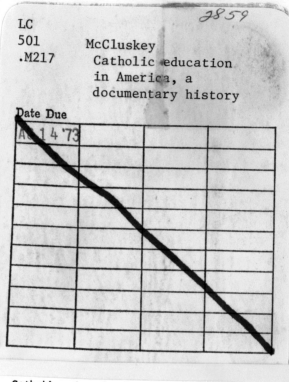

Catholic education in America, a documen
LC501.M217   2859

McCluskey, Neil Gerard
      VRJC/WRIGHT LIBRARY

DEMCO Printed in U.S.A.

CLASSICS IN EDUCATION
Lawrence A. Cremin, General Editor

☆   ☆   ☆

THE REPUBLIC AND THE SCHOOL
Horace Mann on the Education of Free Men
Edited by Lawrence A. Cremin

AMERICAN IDEAS ABOUT ADULT EDUCATION
1710–1951
Edited by C. Hartley Grattan

DEWEY ON EDUCATION
Introduction and Notes by Martin S. Dworkin

THE SUPREME COURT AND EDUCATION
Edited by David Fellman

INTERNATIONAL EDUCATION
A Documentary History
Edited by David G. Scanlon

CRUSADE AGAINST IGNORANCE
Thomas Jefferson on Education
Edited by Gordon C. Lee

CHINESE EDUCATION UNDER COMMUNISM
Edited by Chang-Tu Hu

CHARLES W. ELIOT AND POPULAR EDUCATION
Edited by Edward A. Krug

WILLIAM T. HARRIS ON EDUCATION
(in preparation)
Edited by Martin S. Dworkin

THE EMILE OF JEAN JACQUES ROUSSEAU
Selections
Translated and Edited by William Boyd

THE MINOR EDUCATIONAL WRITINGS OF
JEAN JACQUES ROUSSEAU
Selected and Translated by William Boyd

PSYCHOLOGY AND THE SCIENCE OF EDUCATION
Selected Writings of Edward L. Thorndike
Edited by Geraldine M. Joncich

THE NEW-ENGLAND PRIMER
Introduction by Paul Leicester Ford

BENJAMIN FRANKLIN ON EDUCATION
Edited by John Hardin Best

THE COLLEGES AND THE PUBLIC
1787–1862
Edited by Theodore Rawson Crane

TRADITIONS OF AFRICAN EDUCATION
Edited by David G. Scanlon

NOAH WEBSTER'S AMERICAN SPELLING BOOK
Introductory Essay by Henry Steele Commager

VITTORINO DA FELTRE
AND OTHER HUMANIST EDUCATORS
By William Harrison Woodward
Foreword by Eugene F. Rice, Jr.

DESIDERIUS ERASMUS
CONCERNING THE AIM AND METHOD
OF EDUCATION
By William Harrison Woodward
Foreword by Craig R. Thompson

JOHN LOCKE ON EDUCATION
Edited by Peter Gay

CATHOLIC EDUCATION IN AMERICA
Edited by Neil G. McCluskey, S.J.

Catholic Education
in America

A DOCUMENTARY HISTORY

Edited, with an Introduction and Notes, by

NEIL G. McCLUSKEY, S.J.

CLASSICS IN

No. 21

EDUCATION

BUREAU OF PUBLICATIONS
TEACHERS COLLEGE, COLUMBIA UNIVERSITY

NEW YORK

© 1964 by Teachers College
Columbia University

Library of Congress Catalog Card
Number 64–23907

Printed in the United States of America
by the William Byrd Press, Inc.
Richmond, Virginia

For Teresa and Nan—
and 100,000 other Sisters—
without whom it could not
have happened

Preface

"In 1963," Father McCluskey tells us, "some 5.5 million youngsters, 14 per cent of the nation's school population, were enrolled in 10,633 Catholic elementary schools and 2,502 Catholic secondary schools, representing a $5 billion capital investment and an annual operating cost of $850 million." Even if there were no other reason for widespread interest in Roman Catholic education, these statistics would prove compelling. American Catholics today maintain an educational enterprise second only to the public school system in size and scope; and the inescapable fact is that one cannot understand American education apart from it.

Father McCluskey's effort in the present volume is to trace the intellectual underpinnings of that enterprise, from the earliest pronouncements of Bishop John Carroll in the 1790's to the more recent pastorals of the assembled hierarchy. Following the formulations of his earlier works, *Public Schools and Moral Education* (1958) and *Catholic Viewpoint on Education* (1959), he sees American Catholics caught in a painful dilemma: on the one hand, they have been as eager as their neighbors to give their children the benefits of education; on the other hand, they have felt barred by conscience from sending them to the public school. Virtually all of the documents presented here confront this dilemma in one way or another, seeking viable alternatives to an educational system perceived as blatantly Protestant in the nineteenth century and dangerously secular in the twentieth.

As readers will quickly discover, Father McCluskey's

approach is sympathetic but not uncritical. Though he is obviously appreciative of the contributions of parochial schooling, he sees a number of "less than beneficent outcomes" of the drive for universal Catholic education since 1884, among them, a measure of clerical domination of the schools and a tendency on the part of some clergymen to confuse academic mandate with pastoral charge. Moreover, though he fully understands why leaders of the nineteenth-century Church opted for the principle of every Catholic child in a Catholic school, he makes clear that other alternatives have been available, then and now. Most important, perhaps, he concludes with an eloquent plea for a fresh approach to educational policy-making. "This decade is putting new stresses and strains on both the public school and the Catholic school. These are obviously years of adjustment, both for Catholic education and for public school education. Some of these adjustments will be easier if they are made together." What better statement of the case for dialogue and mutual understanding.

LAWRENCE A. CREMIN

Contents

*Catholic Education
in America*

A DOCUMENTARY HISTORY

America and the Catholic School

By NEIL G. McCLUSKEY, S.J.

When the astute observer looks over the Catholic school system in the United States, he is politely impressed, possibly concerned, and probably puzzled. He is impressed with the sheer dimensions of American Catholic education. In 1963, some 5.5 million youngsters, 14 per cent of the nation's school population, were enrolled in 10,633 Catholic elementary schools and 2,502 Catholic secondary schools, representing a $5 billion capital investment and an annual operating cost of $850 million.[1]

He is possibly concerned lest the spectacular growth of the Catholic system has somehow come at the expense of the public school system. Since World War II, Catholic schools have grown at three times the rate of the public schools. In ten states with a concentrated Catholic population, Catholic schools now educate between 20 and 25 per cent of the total school enrollment. These schools take an even larger share of the school-going population in certain eastern and midwestern cities: in Dubuque, 61 per cent; in Manchester, 52 per cent; in Pittsburgh, 42 per cent; in Philadelphia, 39 per cent; in Buffalo, 38 per cent; in New Orleans, Milwaukee, and Chicago, 33

[1] Unpublished statistics furnished by the Department of Education, National Catholic Welfare Conference, from a report of October 31, 1962.

per cent; in Cleveland and New York, 26 per cent; in St. Louis, 25 per cent; and in Detroit, 23 per cent.[2] Perhaps he has asked himself what effect these separate systems are having on the moral and spiritual tone of the public schools. Are they weakening the academic caliber of public education? Are they the big obstacle to increased federal aid to education? Are they themselves solidly enough financed to ensure education of high quality? Do they make for unity and harmony in the community?

He is probably puzzled as to why Catholic schools exist on the massive scale they do. Do Catholics have such a different idea of the nature of education that they feel compelled to withdraw from the common community effort and set up separate schools for their children? Granting the assumptions, for the most part latent, behind these concerns of the non-Catholic observer, the points raised are valid enough to warrant a fair answer. Moreover, neither Catholic nor non-Catholic can adequately understand and appreciate the place of the Catholic school in modern American society without some knowledge of the thought of the past. The present volume is an attempt partly to meet this need by introducing the reader to a sampling of the important documents that explain Catholic education over the last 175 years.

II

The history of Catholic education in America, like the history of the Church itself, is a story of survival and adaptation. From the first years of the Colonial period to

[2] Bureau of Information, National Catholic Welfare Conference, release of May 1963.

the start of the Revolution, the Catholic Church lived in the catacombs. As a group, Catholics were suspected and feared; as individuals, they lived their lives almost completely outside the principal cultural and political currents. They were denied freedom to worship, to take part in civic affairs, and to educate their children.

Typical of the repressive legislation of the era was Maryland's law of 1704, "An Act to Prevent the Growth of Popery." Among its bristling provisions was one that threatened with deportation any Catholic who should keep school, board students, or instruct children. While disagreeing widely among themselves on religious matters, Anglicans, Congregationalists, Baptists, Methodists, and even Quakers all recognized "the Papist" as the common enemy of all free-born Englishmen, and for such there could be small welcome on the shores of New Canaan. By the dawn of the national period, many of the more onerous disabilities and penalties had been lifted; yet at their constitutional conventions, only four of the original thirteen states gave Catholics the unrestricted right to vote and hold office.

The first attempts to establish Catholic schools were made in Maryland, while this Catholic-founded colony was still a sanctuary of religious freedom. In about 1640, the Jesuit Fathers started a school at St. Mary's City. They began another foundation, probably in 1673, at Newton, a center of underground Catholic activity in Maryland, which by this time had passed from Papist control. Thomas Dongan, the Catholic governor of New York, was responsible for opening a school at Broadway and Wall Street, site of New York's Old Trinity Church, in 1684. These modest beginnings ground to an abrupt halt in the wake of the tightened penal legislation against Catholics, after the Catholic James II had been chased from his throne in 1688. Some fifty years later, the Jesuits tried again at Bohemia Manor, in the northeast corner of Maryland, with a school that remained open until 1765. In this school the sons of many old Catholic families, including the Neales, the Brents, and the Carrolls, began their formal education. Prior to the Revolution, neighboring Pennsylvania had some fifteen Catholic schools, most of them established for the children of German immigrants.

III

In the more congenial climate elsewhere, schools flourished. Massachusetts passed the first general school law in the country, the "Old Deluder Satan" act of 1647. Since that Old Deluder Satan tried to keep Christians from a knowledge of the Scriptures, "as in former times by keeping them in an unknown tongue," this act would thwart him by ordering every township with fifty householders to appoint a teacher and set up a school. Parents of pupils under instruction were to pay the teacher, or, if the town meeting so decided, he could be paid from tax funds. This marks one of the earliest instances in the West in which public authority was recognized as having the right to require the community to establish and maintain schools. The Massachusetts colonists acted on the principle that education is a public concern, even though no clear division then existed between the secular and religious authority of the Commonwealth. One point is clear, however: the overwhelming concern of all New England school laws in that period was the preservation and extension of the Congregational faith. Schools sprang up in the townships, aided by the remarkable homogeneity in language, culture, and religion that the New England communities enjoyed during the seventeenth and eighteenth centuries.

At the beginning of the nineteenth century, the various Protestant churches and sects were still more or less steadfast in their allegiance to the distinctive interpretations of the Bible and patterns of church organization which set them apart. Among the principal influences that began to blunt theological differences and started the parallel process of secularizing American society were the liberal philosophies of the eighteenth century, usually called the Age of the Enlightenment. The rationalism, skepticism, and empiricism of this era challenged the worth of tradition and the need for authority in social, political, and religious thought. A small but influential class, though still identifying themselves as Christians, discarded supernaturally revealed religion and explained the Bible as simply the natural literary expression of ethical truths. They specifically rejected the doctrine of the fall of mankind through Adam's original sin and the consequent need of man for redemption. They extolled the infinite perfectibility of human nature and the limitless power of man to improve his condition on every level through use of his reason. These became basic tenets of Unitarianism.[3]

In retrospect, it is doubtful that the common-school idea could have been accepted as widely as it was without the softening of theological differences brought about by the more liberal currents of early nineteenth-century Protestantism. Differences of belief were relaxed to the point where Congregationalist and Anglican could co-operate in the same educational enterprise. The com-

---

[3] For a fuller treatment of this subject, see Neil G. McCluskey, *Public Schools and Moral Education* (New York: Columbia University Press, 1958), pp. 11–98.

mon school would be Protestant, but would not be under the influence of a particular Protestant sect.

In the 1830's, Horace Mann, one of the first leaders of the common-school movement, argued that Christianity should be taught in the public schools. Children should be given "so much religious instruction as is compatible with the rights of others and with the genius of our government." Mann would leave to parents and guardians any special and peculiar instruction with respect to both politics and theology, and "at last, when the children arrive at years of maturity, . . . commend them to that inviolable prerogative of private judgment and of self-direction, which in a Protestant and a Republican country, is the acknowledged birthright of every human being."

Mann argued that there was a common core of Christian religious beliefs which could be taught in the common school without objection and that the elaboration of this frame could be left to the home and church. Religion was to remain in the public schools, but it was not to be identifiable as Congregational or Episcopal or Methodist. It was simply to be "nonsectarian." When critics charged that he was an enemy of religious instruction in the schools, he explained that he meant only to exclude specific *sectarian* doctrines, or "man-made" creeds, and that to these he was opposing universally accepted Christianity—what he called the "religion of heaven." The fact that Mann's theological positions added up to a doctrine remarkably close to Unitarianism dismayed him not at all. Given the circumstances, almost any approach but Mann's compromise would have meant the disintegration of the common-school movement. He retained the Bible—the traditional symbol of Protestant Christianity—in the schools, "enshielded from harm, by

the great Protestant doctrine of the inviolability of conscience, the right and sanctity of private judgment, without note or interpreter." Mann appealed to the classical
Protestant principle that "the Bible is the acknowledged
expositor of Christianity," and "in strictness, Christianity
has no other authoritative expounder."

IV

The second factor which powered the public school
movement was an increased awareness of what American
democracy had to mean in practice. The presidential
victory of Andrew Jackson in 1828 marked the real beginning of popular democracy in this country. The cul-
tivated aristocracy that had led the Colonial struggle and
created the nation retained a class outlook on popular
education. Not uncommon was the attitude Thomas
Jefferson recorded in his *Notes on the State of Virginia*
(1781; published 1785). To diffuse knowledge more generally among the people, he proposed a chain of widely
dispersed elementary schools; "the boy of best genius" in
each would be given further education at one of twenty
grammar schools. From each of these, a student would be
selected, after a one- or two-year trial, to continue for
another six years, and "by this means twenty of the
best geniuses will be raked from the rubbish annually,
and be instructed, at the public expense, so far as the
grammar schools go."[4]

But Jefferson and many other leaders saw that the distinctive character of the republican form of government
demanded an informed and literate citizenry as its solid
foundation. If the monarchical and class forms of Old

[4] Saul K. Padover, ed., *The Complete Jefferson* (New York: Tudor
Publishing Co., 1943), p. 667.

World government were no longer applicable to the American republic, then the people had to be educated to the level where they could participate intelligently in political decisions. This, in turn, necessitated universal schooling. Such was the incessant theme of Horace Mann and other leaders in the common-school movement.

When Mann and the other pioneers came on the scene, they were aided in their undertaking by the growing feeling that education was not something which the civil authority should merely encourage, but rather a direct responsibility of the State. This gradual change in attitude came about for a number of reasons, none more immediately compelling than the increased awareness that the church-sponsored schools and private academies were failing to provide for all children. Commonly, the children of the better classes were the only ones for whom adequate provision was made in religious schools.

When referring to the opening of "George-Town College" in his letter of 1792 to the Catholic people of the United States, Bishop John Carroll said: "I earnestly wish, dear brethren, that as many of you, as are able, would send your sons to this school of letters and virtue. I know and lament, that the expense will be too great for many families, and that their children must be deprived of the immediate benefit of this institution. . . ."[5] And in 1829, the Catholic bishops wrote in a similar vein: "How well would it be, if your means and opportunities permitted, were you at this period to commit your children to the care of those whom we have for their special fitness, placed over our seminaries and our female religious institutions?"[6]

Even during the first half of the nineteenth century, the

[5] See p. 48.
[6] See p. 55.

school was still looked upon pretty much as a private
venture, ordinarily the business of the church or of
private initiative with some sort of ecclesiastical super-
vision, undertaken for the benefit of those who could
afford it or profit from it. When the drive for universal
education got under way, however, the evangelical sects—
mainly the Methodists and Baptists—were overtaking
the older Protestant churches in number and influence.
The newer groups had no tradition of church-controlled
schools and found little difficulty in accepting government
control of education.

V

It is simply assumed today that the State has the right to
establish and operate schools, but this assumption is
something that arrived on the social scene rather late.
When at the St. Paul meeting of the NEA in 1890 Archbishop John Ireland voiced his own conviction that the
question of the State's right in education had been settled,
many people, including certain of his episcopal con-
freres, would have sharply disagreed. It was not settled at
all, according to Bishop Bernard McQuaid, who said:
"The Catholic is unwilling to transfer the responsibility
of the education of his children to the state. His conscience informs him that the state is an incompetent
agent to fulfil his parental duties."[7]

This view was not held among Catholics alone; a large
number of others shared it. McQuaid could quote in his
favor the authority of Herbert Spencer, who had written:

In the same way that our definition of state duty forbids the
State to administer religion or charity, so likewise does it

[7] *The Public School Question* (Boston: Duffy and Co., 1876), p. 9.

forbid the State to administer education. Inasmuch as the
taking away by Government, of more of a man's property than
is needful for maintaining his rights, is an infringement and
therefore a reversal of the government's function toward him,
and inasmuch as the taking away of his property to educate
his own or other people's children is not needful for the
maintaining of his rights; the taking away of his property
is wrong. . . .[8]

One of the authorities on whom Ireland leaned, in
asserting the State's direct right to educate, was Dr.
Thomas Bouquillon, Belgian-born professor of moral
science at the Catholic University of America. The appearance in 1891 of his pamphlet *Education: To Whom
Does It Belong?* was not just a bow to the social reality;
it was the somewhat tardy explication of a principle
long implicit in Catholic teaching, that is, that within
reason, the State has a right to utilize all the means necessary to achieve its legitimate end in any stage of society.[9]
Nonetheless, the pamphlet's appearance caused consterna-
tion and quickly drew rejoinders.

Bouquillon's Catholic critics could point to the long
series of pastoral letters issued by the American bishops,
not a single one of which even hinted that the State had
a direct right in education. The most prestigious of the
councils, the Third Plenary of Baltimore, had stated:
"The three great educational agencies are the home, the
Church, and the school," a view which seemed pointedly
to ignore the State. The prevailing sentiment among
Catholics was expressed in *The American Catholic Quarterly Review:* "The State has the right and the duty to
encourage good education; but its right to educate is but

8 *Ibid.,* p. 7.
9 A thorough treatment of this point can be found in Thomas
Dubay, *Philosophy of the State as Educator* (Milwaukee, Wis.: The
Bruce Publishing Co., 1959).

a Masonic invention."[10] And the Bishop of Trenton had put it even more strongly in saying "that the idea that the state has a right to teach . . . is not a Christian idea. It is a pagan one. . . ."[11]

A distinguished American historian has pointed out that up to the time of the struggle by Archbishop Hughes and the Catholic community of New York for tax support of Catholic schools, "Catholics and non-Catholics had been in essential agreement regarding parental responsibility for the education of children. But with the common school awakening, the gradual disappearance of religious teaching and atmosphere from the public schools, and the new conception that their work was primarily secular and designed to fit the youth of the land for the duties of citizenship, the older idea that education was a parental responsibility gave way to the belief that it was an enterprise of the state."[12]

The general Catholic reluctance (and that of many others) during the nineteenth century to view the State as anything but a substitute for parents delinquent in their duty of educating the child must be understood against a backdrop of radical social changes in Europe. One such change was the State's encroachment on the regulation of marriage. From time immemorial the Church had had sole jurisdiction over the bond of matrimony. Marriage was at the same time a contract and a sacrament, and both were regulated sacredly by the Church. The jurisdiction of the State extended only to

10 P. Bayma, "The Liberalistic View of the Public School Question," *The American Catholic Quarterly Review*, II (1877), 17.

11 Quoted in Daniel F. Reilly, *The School Controversy (1891–1893)* (Washington, D.C.: The Catholic University of America Press, 1943), p. 107.

12 Merle Curti, *The Social Ideas of American Educators* (Paterson, N.J.: Pageant Books, 1959), p. 349.

the civil aspects of a marriage, to such items as dowries, inheritances, legitimacy of succession, etc. After the breakup of Christian unity in the sixteenth century, the Protestant churches generally continued this division of ecclesiastical and secular jurisdiction. It is true that in the Preface to his Catechism of 1529, Luther had argued that the regulation of marriage belonged to the State, because it was a secular business (*"ein weltlich Geschaft," "ein weltlich Ding"*). Other theologians of the Reformation, however, did not agree with him.

But in the last two decades of the eighteenth century, the secularization of marriage was partially or wholly effected in all the principal countries of Europe. Church authority was set aside, and the principle was enunciated that the secular power has the sole competence in regulating the marriage contract. In France during the 1790's, the men of the Revolution organized a complete republican liturgy to replace the Catholic nuptial ceremonies. In fact, Robespierre carried through the Convention a law establishing a "Feast of Conjugal Love," upon which day marital unions could be solemnized.

It is scarcely any wonder, then, that men who recalled these changes feared that once education came under state control, it, like marriage, would be secularized. Education and marriage are inseparably linked, and the secular and religious authorities have a valid concern for both, a point to which we shall later return.

VI

Catholics in America were caught up in a painful dilemma. They were as eager to send their children to school as their Protestant neighbors, but in good conscience, they could not. Literacy, knowledge, skills—

these were the steps to the full sharing of all that was the American dream. But the common schools had not been designed with Roman Catholic children in mind. These schools, for whose support Catholics were taxed, smacked strongly of Protestantism, with their Protestant books, hymns, prayers, and, above all, their Protestant Bible. Catholics sought to alleviate their plight in two ways. They asked that Catholic youngsters be excused from classroom reading of the Protestant Bible and similar devotional practices and that school taxes paid by Catholics be used to educate their children in church schools.

In the matter of Bible reading, Catholics found no legal redress. On the contrary, strong legal support for the religious status quo in the public schools was supplied by an 1854 ruling of the Maine Supreme Court (*Donahue* v. *Richards*), permitting school officials to require the reading of the King James version of the Bible, a precedent which was not successfully challenged until near the close of the century.

The effort by Catholics to obtain a share of the tax money collected for the schools likewise failed. Their brief was set forth with dignity and clarity by the New York Catholics in 1840. Speaking for the entire Catholic community, the spokesmen informed the Board of Aldermen that as Catholics:

They bear, and are willing to bear, their portion of every common burden; and feel themselves entitled to a participation in every common benefit.

This participation, they regret to say, has been denied them for years back, in reference to Common School Education in the city of New York, except on conditions with which their conscience, and, as they believe their duty to God, did not, and do not leave them at liberty to comply.[13]

13 See p. 66.

One result of this Catholic agitation was that New York City's common schools were shortly taken over by the State from the private group calling itself the Public School Society. Yet this was no solution to the root problem of parental freedom of choice in education. The move was, however, a large step toward the inevitable secularization of the schools. The pattern of no funds for denominationally controlled schools was set—and has endured, with minor exceptions, down to the present day.

The great Protestant majority was easily persuaded that Catholic efforts to eliminate the Protestant Bible from the schools and to get public money for their own schools represented a concerted attack on the foundations of the republic. It was simply taken for granted that the Bible and the flag symbolized America and that an attack on one was an assault on the other. Since nativism looked to Protestant Christianity as the source and guarantee of its moral influence, it was easy enough to turn Catholic efforts for accommodation in the area of education into an occasion for a crusade.[14]

The voices of the moderates from either side who were willing to discuss compromises were quickly drowned out. Bigots and extremists—at times on the Catholic side, too—carried the day. The 1830's saw the burning of the Charleston Convent and Maria Monk's "Awful Disclosures." In the 1850's, there were the Philadelphia riots, the demonstrations during the tour of the pope's representative, Archbishop Bedini, the tarring and feathering of the Jesuit John Bapst, the Massachusetts law for

[14] In fact, the word appears in the title of the most competent study yet made of this period: Ray A. Billington, *The Protestant Crusade, 1800–1860* (New York: The Macmillan Co., 1938).

the inspection of the convents of nuns, and the riots and bloodshed of Louisville's "Bloody Monday." The Civil War broke up the politically powerful Know-Nothing movement, but the forces of nativism banded together again in the 1880's to form the American Protective Association.

This is the dark side of the story of the public school movement and reflects little credit on the land of religious liberty.[15] In fairness, however, as Orestes A. Brownson tried to explain to his fellow Catholics, Protestant antipathy toward things Catholic was a complex matter.[16] With the arrival on American shores of hundreds of thousands of Irish and German Catholics, the name "Catholic" began to conjure up much more than simply a religious affiliation. These people were not just Catholics, but foreigners with a different look and a strange accent to them. Their cheap labor flooding the market posed an economic threat. They were people of the ghetto, the slum, and the saloon. When they refused to patronize the common schools and set up separate institutions for their children, sometimes schools where a foreign tongue was the principal language (as in the case of the German schools), perceptive Protestants saw them as a menace to the American way.[17]

[15] As the Catholic-Protestant polemic fades farther and farther away, the chances increase that more historians and fewer apologetes will turn their attention to the dreadfully neglected field of American education.

[16] See pp. 115–116.

[17] Ireland, Gibbons, and Spalding were more perspicacious here than the Germanizing bishops of the Midwest. Their idea was to "Americanize" the Church, hence proving again its catholicity. This included a reasonable acceptance of the American school as something good and worth coming to terms with. For Ireland's views, see pp. 127–150; for Spalding's, see pp. 166–174.

VII

But the Protestants of the nation had—and have—their
own dilemma to face. In opposing Catholic influence in
the public schools, they were forced to stand by and
watch helplessly, as all religious influence disappeared
and a totally secular philosophy moved in. Traditionally,
the American people have come to look upon the schools
as the most efficient means of transmitting to children
the public philosophy which undergirds our society.
They have insisted that the school assume a proper
responsibility for developing the child's character or,
to phrase it for the modern ear, for inculcating moral
and spiritual values. But the history of the public school
has made it plain that this mandate, however feasible in
the past, is impossible to discharge any longer. The common school is assigned a responsibility for character
education, but whatever Christian consensus formerly
existed as to the nature of this chore has long since disappeared.

In the 1840's, it was relatively easy: character formation was based upon the morality and inspiration of the
Christian Bible. In teaching religion the public school
was not to favor any one sect in the community but to
inculcate the generally agreed upon moral and religious
truths of all Protestants, as given in the Bible. This compromise was originally intended to safeguard the rights
of conscience and the constitutional exercise of religious
freedom by individuals, as well as to protect the equal
position of the Protestant churches and sects in the
common schools. There was no question of a philosophy
of education hostile to religious teaching as such.

In the mid-nineteenth century, however, important
figures in the educational world began to argue with
success that by its very nature the school is completely

secular and hence incompetent to enter the sphere of religious education. This position was not dictated by hostility toward religion or religious education; it was rather concerned with the most appropriate occasion for efficient instruction in religion and with safeguarding the rights of private conscience. (In effect, this position also provided a logical basis for denying a share of public funds to religious schools.) In method, spirit, and content, it was urged, secular truth is necessarily antagonistic to the acquisition of religious truth, to the extent that the two cannot be taught under the same roof. Moreover, those who argued this position frankly acknowledged the religious fragmentation of society. Thus, Bishop Spalding could say: "I am willing to assume and to accept as a fact that our theological differences make it impossible to introduce the teaching of any religious creed into the public school. I take the system as it is,— that is, as a system of secular education. . . ."[18]

The current understanding of "secular," however, is vastly different from its meaning for the men of Bishop Spalding's day. Until quite recent years, moral and spiritual values were universally assumed to be rooted in some kind of religious value system. Despite sectarian differences, American leadership could count on general acceptance of a theistically based natural law, upon which was reared the unity of what men considered a "Christian" nation. This included belief in the existence of a Creator, who was the source of the justice and the rights defined in the nation's first great political documents.

The naturalist philosophy of scientific humanism propounded in this century by John Dewey and others has had much to do with emptying the concept of "secular"

[18] See p. 167.

of its theistic-natural law content. Dewey advanced a "scientific" substitute for the traditional concept of religion, which he judged would be more in keeping with the exigencies of modern democratic society. Since his empirical pragmatist philosophy limited reality to the natural order, no place was left for supernatural religion either within or outside the school.

Today, the ethics of total secularism or scientism have largely replaced the moral values of the Judaeo-Christian tradition as the basis for character formation in public education. It has become impossible for the schools in most areas to teach what many parents believe should be taught their children. Parents and church people have yielded step by step to the importuning of minority groups, not simply pushing to remove all religious influence from the schools, but working to erect the kind of legal "wall" between the churches and the state school that would make it impossible for church groups to collaborate in any way with the public schools.

To assert this is not to ignore the central problem, namely, the limitations inherent in the idea of one *common* school serving a religiously pluralistic society. The coexistence within the same society of groups holding fundamentally different views regarding the nature and destiny of man has made for an impasse in the approach to the moral side of education. For in the final analysis, moral and spiritual values are built upon what men hold as ultimate or supreme in life. Obviously, it is only in an ideal society, wherein men agree freely and completely about ultimate values, that a common approach to the moral side of education can be readily found.

For a long period in our history, there was some basis for a general agreement on values and their sanctions.

The Old World legacy of Greco-Roman natural law and of the central religious concepts of the Judaeo-Christian tradition was almost universally accepted and was widely operative in American society. There was agreement on what constitutes the basis and general content of a Christian philosophy of character education, despite quarrels over the version of the Bible upon which this should be based. However, the fragmentation of the Protestant churches multiplied differences over dogma both among Protestants themselves and with the Catholics, whose increasing numbers each decade gave them a louder voice. Non-European religious groups established themselves. New groups arose whose ultimates derived from a secular and humanistic rather than a Christian tradition. All these factors entered into the historical process which has resulted in the official secularization of large sectors of American public education.

VIII

The compromise approach of Horace Mann contained the principle of its own dissolution. The precious little common ground that once existed among Unitarians, Methodists, Congregationalists, Catholics, Jews, and deists gradually eroded. The positive doctrinal elements regarding church organization, sacraments, and the mission of Christ had to be strained out of the common-school religion piece by piece to avoid offending dissenters. Such a process of attrition inevitably worked to the advantage of groups holding a minimum of positive doctrine or none at all. A blandly Christian flavor that contented Unitarians could only dismay Congregationalists and Episcopalians. The soup in time got so thin that it pleased no palate. Belief in God, the Golden

VERNON REGIONAL
JUNIOR COLLEGE LIBRARY

Rule, and the Bible were all that long survived this process of disintegration.

When the Bible in the classroom became an object of contention between Protestants and Catholics, and later between Christians and non-Christians, the courts banned Bible-reading in eight states. The 1963 ruling of the United States Supreme Court has stopped the practice in thirteen other states, where it was required, and in twenty-five more, where it was permitted. In recent years, public school exercises formally expressing belief in God have also been under steady attack. The *Engel* v. *Vitale* decision of the same tribunal in 1962 ended the optional recitation of a privately composed prayer in New York State. Yet the process of total secularization of the common school has been a consistent one—the working out of an inner logic whose final outcome is not yet in view. In some measure due to Catholic intransigence, the compromise idea that began life so hopefully in the 1840's has become bankrupt. America's public schools are no longer either Protestant or Christian. They are no longer religiously oriented. They are officially secular.

Faced with the ultimate question of whether religion is the starting point and essence of true education, the public school has had to adopt a theoretical neutrality between those who believe in the God of the Western tradition and those who do not. Yet the public school is not really neutral, for it gives an equivalent denial to the question by actually taking another starting point and aiming at another goal. What is worse, the public school, by default, facilitates the entry of a naturalist religion of democracy, or secularist cult of society, into the vacuum, so that only the child from a secularist family can feel perfectly at home in the common public schools. By default, civic or political virtue has become practically the exclusive goal of public school education. In other words, these schools exist primarily to produce good citizens. It can be granted that within a religiously divided society a common school by itself cannot easily achieve a broader goal. The point to be made here, however, is that the philosophy of public school education is being dictated by those forces in society which, wanting no other goal for it, have nearly succeeded in quarantining the public school from the churches and church-related organizations.[19]

In retrospect, it is only fair to point out that secularists are not the only ones responsible for what took place in the public schools. Sectarian bitterness and denominational jealousies greatly neutralized the influence of religion in the schools. The resulting impasse has facilitated the entry into the schools of a philosophy of moral and spiritual values completely divorced from religion, while advocates of a climate favorable to a religiously based moral and spiritual program in the public schools have been able to glorify the ideal of the uncommitted mind and the uncommitted conscience, or that vaguest of all ideals—humanitarianism. As a result, the American public school is now unable or unwilling to take a stand on, or perhaps even to confront, the central questions regarding the meaning of man: his origin, his purpose, his destiny. Even with all the good will in the world, public school teachers are less and less free, not simply to answer, but often even to ask, the great questions about God, conscience, duty, rights, and the future life.

[19] See Neil G. McCluskey, *Catholic Viewpoint on Education* (Garden City, N.Y.: Doubleday-Image, 1962), p. 53. The chapter on "The Evolution of the Secular School" discusses this problem.

IX

The central problem, we repeat, is the contradiction inherent in the very idea of one common school attempting to serve a religiously pluralistic society. Correlative to this problem has always been the place of the independent, church-related school in the total scheme of things. There are those who resent the growth of the Catholic school and regard it as a threat to the public school. When they oppose any kind of public support for Catholic schools, they have recourse to that argument which calls parochial school education "divisive" or "un-American" or "undemocratic." In reality, the opposition is not to the support of these schools but to their very existence. At times, these opponents of Catholic education have used the word "boycott" to stigmatize the choice Catholic parents freely make between the public school and the Catholic school. Their initial assumption is that the state-established secular school has some claim on the primary allegiance of all citizens. In their book any citizen who, compelled by conscience, chooses to exercise his natural right to patronize his own school becomes guilty of disloyalty to a state enterprise.

Yet this attitude bespeaks a strange reversal of values honored in both the Judaeo-Christian and the American traditions. There is a primacy of spiritual values over the purely secular, and consequently there is a priority of choice in education, which is part of the religious freedom of parents. This is the oft-recurring theme of the pastoral letters of the American bishops.

One of the most complete statements of the entire philosophy of Catholic education is found in the encyclical letter of Pope Pius XI, "The Christian Education of Youth" (*Divini Illius Magistri*).[20] The starting point in the Catholic idea of education is the reality of the supernatural as revealed through, and in the person of, Jesus Christ the Saviour. The Catholic belief that man is a creature of God destined to share in the divine life answers the two questions upon which every philosophy of education is built: What is man? What is his purpose? This sharing in the divine life begins at the moment of baptism, when sanctifying grace and the virtues of faith, hope, and charity—man's supernatural faculties, as it were—are infused into his soul. That life, which begins on earth through faith, is perfected in a beatific union with God in glory hereafter. For a believer, this truth is not only the ultimate purpose and final objective of education; it is the theological integrating principle, the philosophical guide, and the basis of sanctions in the moral order.

Needless to add, there are millions of American Protestants who are as deeply convinced of these truths as any Catholic. Yet they can no longer look to the public school for help in passing on to their children even as primary a truth as the existence of a personal God or the reality of the supernatural order. Ironically, the Protestant churches have been put in a position where they must side with the State against institutional religion and promote secular rather than religious values in the schools.

As American society has taken on more and more a secular orientation, certain truths of the Christian philosophy of education have been pushed unobtrusively into the background. Because the State now plays the

[20] The encyclical has been published in convenient pamphlet form by the America Press, 920 Broadway, New York 10, N.Y.

dominant role in education, there are public school apologists and philosophers of education who operate on the assumption that the school and the schoolchild exist primarily for the State. They must be continually reminded that this assumption can be valid only in a totalitarian state, whether one selects the Republic of Plato or the Cuba of Castro.[21]

By way of contrast, the Catholic Church still teaches that since education is coextensive with human life itself, different agencies in society share rights and responsibilities in this broad field. For man is born into three subsocieties of the larger society: the family, civil society (including the State), and the Church. Each has distinct rights, but all should be properly ordered to ensure balance and harmony within the total educational process.

When the religious dimension in education is absent, the natural harmony of the child's formation is upset. The Sunday school approach, upon which Protestants generally have relied, has not been a conspicuous success in recent decades, any more than parallel Catholic efforts to teach formal religion outside the public school.

X

Historically, since the Catholic youngster was not made to feel at home in the public school, he went to his own

[21] Whenever the occasion has offered itself, the United States Supreme Court has reaffirmed the American principle that "the child is not the mere creature of the State" (*Pierce* v. *Society of Sisters,* 1925) and that "the custody, care and nurture of the child reside first in the parents" (*Prince* v. *Massachusetts,* 1944). Unambiguous support for the primacy of the family right is likewise to be found in the Universal Declaration of Human Rights, proclaimed by the General Assembly of the United Nations (December 10, 1948): "Parents have a prior right to choose the kind of education that shall be given to their children" (Article 26, par. 3).

school, wherever possible. After the failure of the 1840 effort to have the New York parochial schools receive public support, Catholics began to expend their interest and energy almost exclusively on Catholic parochial and private schools, leaving the public schools as semi-Protestant domain.

In the decade after the Civil War, popular education began to take hold everywhere. In 1880, public school enrollment reached 1 million for the first time, but in 1900, it soared to 15 million, and in 1920, to 21 million. Under the impetus of the school legislation passed in 1884 by the Third Plenary Council of Baltimore, Catholic school enrollment likewise began to mount. At the turn of the century, there were 854,523 pupils in Catholic schools, and by 1920, this number had more than doubled to 1.8 million. The current enrollment in Catholic schools is 5.5 million, or 14 per cent of the nation's total elementary- and secondary-school population. But this achievement has not been without a price—in more than dollars. Thoughtful leaders within the Church are calling for a reappraisal of certain traditional practices and policies, for American Catholics also confront a period of decision.

XI

Since the Third Council of Baltimore, an ideal of Catholic education has been held up: "Every Catholic child in a Catholic school." After eighty years of almost superhuman exertion to realize this ideal, it remains as distant as it has always been. Better than five million of today's Catholic youngsters—two-thirds of those of high-school age and about 40 per cent of those of elementary-school age—are not enrolled in Catholic schools. Given the

current framework of operation, these children are not
going to get even a partial Catholic schooling. In fact, the
number of the unaccommodated will be greater each
successive year.

In July of 1963, the chairman of the school board of
the Archdiocese of Cincinnati, Auxiliary Bishop Paul F.
Leibold, announced that because the archdiocese faced
a financial crisis, it would probably be necessary to drop
the first four grades from Cincinnati Catholic schools.
In any event, no further school construction would be
undertaken until there was an adequate supply of trained
teachers and funds to compensate them properly. A
few weeks earlier, the Rochester diocese had announced that after September there would be a ban for
the immediate future on the building of new Catholic
schools and on expansion of existing schools. A year
earlier, the Cardinal Archbishop of St. Louis had laid
down a similar policy for his archdiocese. The bishops
of Saginaw, Spokane, Kansas City, Fargo, Richmond,
and Green Bay have all been forced to adjust to the
shortage of teachers and classrooms by eliminating one
or more grades from their schools.[22]

What has happened? Have the archbishops and
bishops of these dioceses abandoned the ideal of Catholic education? Has the drive for Catholic schools finally
run out of steam? Not at all. To begin with, the parents'
demand for Catholic education for their youngsters has
not slackened in the least. A spot check of eight diocesan

[22] On March 5, 1964, Archbishop Karl J. Alter announced the
discontinuation of the first grade in all primary schools of the
Roman Catholic Archdiocese of Cincinnati as of September 1964.
The following day, the pastor of a Roman Catholic church of a
suburb of Milwaukee said that he would eliminate the first four
grades from his parochial school starting September 1965. See *New
York Times*, March 6, 1964, pp. 1, 5; March 7, 1964, p. 21.

school systems in the summer of 1963 revealed that principals had been forced to turn away some thirty-seven thousand applicants—nineteen thousand for elementary and eighteen thousand for secondary grades.[23]

With some exceptions, the quality of Catholic elementary and secondary education, like that of the public schools, is steadily improving, and for many of the same reasons.[24] Year after year, the total enrollment continues to rise. No, Catholic leadership in the United States is not doing an about-face but is at last confronting some of the hard realities of the present and the inviting challenges of the future. Despite the impressive accomplishments of the Catholic schools over the past eighty years— and they are truly many—Catholic leadership is beginning to realize that some of the successful patterns of the past have served their purpose. New approaches, new emphases, new methods are called for in order to continue achieving the perennial goals of Catholic education.

It is taking nothing from the leadership of the past, from the men of courage and vision who were the architects of today's monument, to enumerate four less than beneficent outcomes of the drive since 1884 for universal Catholic education in this country. They are: (1) Clerical domination of the schools; (2) Overcommitment to

[23] Reported by the Bureau of Information, National Catholic Welfare Conference, as: Brooklyn, 7,027 (turned away); Pittsburgh, 6,767; Rockville Centre, 5,724; San Francisco, 5,534; Buffalo, 3,750; Baltimore, 3,650; Chicago, 2,837.

[24] Catholic schools meet the requirements of state education laws and also try to measure their performance by standards laid down by the voluntary accrediting agencies. In the New England Association, for example, 16.1 per cent of the Catholic schools are accredited as against 9.3 per cent of the public schools; in the Middle States Association, 22 per cent of the Catholic schools are accredited and 25.8 per cent of the public schools.

the elementary school; (3) Confusion of the academic mandate and the pastoral charge; (4) Substitution of the school for the family and Church as the primary agent in the religious formation of the child.

XII

From earliest times, the conduct of Catholic education in America has necessarily been almost exclusively the charge of the clergy and the religious orders. There was little alternative and large precedent for this policy. From the financial point of view, there simply would not have been money even for the modest salaries that teachers generally receive. Moreover, there is a rich tradition of clerical and religious activity in education. In many European countries the schools of the religious teaching groups, such as the Brothers of the Christian Schools and the Jesuits, have always been held in the highest regard. A convent-school education for girls has always been considered by affluent Catholics (and often non-Catholics) to confer a special cachet. Consequently, congregations of teaching nuns and Brothers were invited over from Europe. Dozens of native American congregations of Sisters were founded. The services of these dedicated men and women made it possible to open schools on a scale undreamed of.

Until 1945, there seemed to be a steady, though always insufficient, supply of vocations, especially to the sisterhoods, but since then the demand has galloped far ahead of the supply. In addition, the standards of teacher preparation for all schools have been firmed up considerably, so that it now takes longer to train a teaching nun. At one time there may have been basis for the criticism that many religious women teachers began their class-

room careers without collegiate and professional training equivalent to that of their counterparts in the public
schools. It was true that many congregations of Sisters
had the practice of putting teachers to work after only
two years of concentrated preparation. These young
teachers would then take additional professional courses
in summer schools, eventually completing the work for
a college degree.

There was always some justification for this practice,
which, until a few decades ago, was not uncommon
among teachers going into public schools. The fact that
the young Sister lived in a convent community of veteran
teachers and was able to profit from close, friendly su-
pervision and counseling could be viewed as more than
adequate compensation for any delay in taking extra
courses in formal pedagogy.

The establishment in 1953 of the National Sister Formation Conference, however, has worked a quiet revolution among the women's congregations. The idea of
the Conference is, as one leader has stated it, "that
Sisters doing active works in our own times need a long
and careful spiritual formation, a general intellectual
training which will equip them for a rich personal life
and an effective social leadership, and a precise professional preparation which will make them the equals
or superiors of lay people doing the same kind of
work."[25] That this farseeing policy is being successfully
implemented is attested by the temporary halt to
school expansion in many dioceses. The mainstay of
the Catholic elementary and secondary school remains
the teaching nun. In 1961, some one hundred thousand
Sisters were in the classroom. Nearly fifty thousand lay

[25] Sister Mary Emil, I.H.M., then executive secretary of the Sister
Formation Conferences, in *America*, XCVI (January 12, 1957), 412.

teachers, an average of between three and four for every one of the thirteen thousand Catholic schools, were teaching alongside them. But most remarkable of all, the percentage of lay teachers in elementary schools has leaped from 7.1 in 1950 to 29.5 in 1961, and on the secondary-school level, from 16.6 in 1950 to 26.7 in 1961.

Though lay teachers in significant numbers arrived late, they are here to stay—to the great strengthening of the Catholic system. Obviously school population pressures had most to do with altering the old pattern, but new attitudes in the Catholic community would have brought about the change regardless. In planning any future expansion in Catholic education, the key figure will be the lay teacher. Qualified religious teachers will, of course, continue to shoulder much of the burden, but the lay teacher will also make his own rich contribution to the academic ideals and religious tone of the schools. And finally, it may be pointed out that the increased presence of the laity in the parochial school will mean a lessening of the mistrust the strongly sectarian nature of these institutions once inspired in the community.

XIII

When in 1884 the Third Plenary Council of Baltimore ordered that a school was to be established near every church "within two years," the school envisaged was an elementary school, the type of school which satisfied the needs and ambitions of the overwhelming majority of Americans of that era. Eighty years later, Catholic emphasis still remains on the elementary school, despite the enormous changes in the schooling pattern of American society. In 1880, an American averaged less than three full years of schooling, but the average American of today has completed ten years and six months.

It is patent that the high school has replaced the elementary school as the center of loyalties and educational influences for the American citizen. Moreover, even this is changing. Increasingly, the thirteenth and fourteenth years—junior college—are becoming a normal part of the educational pattern.

It can be argued whether the earlier or later years are psychologically more important in the child's formation. But there is no argument over the fact that today the secondary school and the college play a much more dominant role in the life of a young person than does the elementary school. In the case of the young child, his recreation, hobbies, and amusements, his physical weakness, affections, and sense of dependence naturally keep him close to his home and family. During these delicate years, the school is obviously important in helping to mold character, but its influence is less than that of the family. Once a youngster begins high school, however, the distribution of his waking hours alone gives the school the ascendancy in influence. Now, not only are classes and studies and friendships centered at school, but the ever-increasing whirl of co-curricular and extra-curricular activities engages the high-school student six days of each week and more. Thirty years ago, the platform orator could nostalgically refer to his happy childhood at P.S. 64 or the Evergreen Grammar School. Today, one never identifies with the elementary school as he does with the high school or the college.

Current shortages of classrooms and teachers have forced Catholic leaders to face this problem squarely. As president-general of the National Catholic Educa-

tional Association, the Archbishop of Baltimore, the Most
Rev. Lawrence J. Shehan, said in his keynote address to
the national convention:

In certain localities where with existing plant, personnel and
resources it seems impossible to provide full Catholic education for all Catholic children, the question has been raised
about the advisability of offering to every child Catholic education at a certain level. Since young children are more completely under the control of their parents, since it is common
experience that during the younger years attention and interest
can be held by extracurricular religious instruction, and since
neither of these conditions holds true during the year of
adolescence, thought might well be given to a plan to provide
all children with Catholic education, say from the seventh to
the twelfth grade. At least we would have nothing to lose and
perhaps much to gain if carefully planned and observed
experiments were tried in areas where the full course of
Catholic education cannot be offered to all children at the
present time.[26]

The overcommitment of the Catholic Church in the
United States to the elementary school has diverted
money, personnel, and attention from the secondary
schools. Few dioceses can currently accommodate in their
high schools the yearly graduating classes from the elementary schools. Back in 1900, about 10 per cent of the
total population of high-school age was attending secondary schools, and three out of four high-school graduates continued on to college. In 1961, 90.2 per cent of
high-school age youngsters was in high school, and more
than half the graduating class went on to college. Many
dioceses are unwilling or unable to make the adjustment
called for by these drastic changes in the American

[26] National Catholic Educational Association, *Bulletin,* Report of
the Proceedings and Addresses—Fifty-sixth Annual Meeting, LVI
(August, 1959), 40.

school pattern, with the result that most of their high-school age youngsters are in public schools.

If the development of secondary-school education has flagged because of preoccupation with elementary schools, what should be said of the plight of American Catholic colleges and universities? Although less valid now than in 1941, D. W. Brogan's candid appraisal that "in no modern Western society is the intellectual prestige of Catholicism lower than in the country where, in such respects as wealth, numbers, and strength of organization, it is so powerful" could never have been made if the colleges and universities had been supported by the Catholic community.[27]

Since the building of elementary schools on a massive scale drained the Catholic purse, there was not a great deal of money left for the support of higher education. With a handful of exceptions, the Catholic colleges and universities have received practically no financial support from the dioceses. As a consequence, even the six universities and twenty-five or so colleges that have achieved some stature in the academic community have not yet realized their full promise.

XIV

The third by-product of the heavy Catholic commitment to the elementary school has been gradually diminishing in recent years. This is the confusion of the academic mandate and the pastoral charge.

Some would explain the rationale of the Catholic school by saying simply that it exists "to save souls." Al-

[27] *U. S. A.: An Outline of the Country, Its People and Institutions* (London: Oxford University Press, 1941), p. 65. On later study-visits, the distinguished Cambridge historian remarked on the enormous improvement in this area.

though this is correct, it is seriously misleading. It would be just as true to say that the purpose of Catholic hospitals, youth clubs, summer camps, and veterans' organizations is "to save souls." The saving of souls is too general an explanation of the school's purpose and fails to indicate its specific objective, that which distinguishes the school from the hospital, the youth club, the summer camp, and the veterans' organization. Each of these institutions has its own immediate and distinctive end or purpose. Since the saving of souls is the purpose of all these agencies, it can describe only the school's ultimate purpose, a purpose it necessarily shares in the absolute order with all human undertakings.

Could it not be objected, however, that in operating schools the Catholic Church is simply trying to make good Catholics, and that the priests, Brothers, Sisters, and even lay people who teach in them are agents of the Roman Catholic Church?

This objection is based on a confusion between the purpose of the work itself and the purpose or *motive* of the worker. Education is education, and a school is a school, regardless of the motives of those conducting it. In other words, the school retains its nature and basic purpose despite the reasons the Church or the State may have for sponsoring educational activity. The State enters into education because it wants its citizens to have an adequate knowledge of their civic duties and privileges, and to make sure they reach the level of physical, intellectual, and moral culture required for the common good. The Church establishes schools in order that these same persons, as members of her communion, will better acquire the supreme integrating principle of supernatural wisdom for ordering the knowledge, skills, and attitudes they obtain. Neither the motive of the State nor the motive of the Church alters the essential nature of the school. The failure to make the distinction between the agent's motivation and the intrinsic formality of the work itself can lead to two different attitudes, both, in the final analysis, irrational.

In the one case, the result is the contrived dilemma wherein one is confronted with the stark choice of flag or cross, fatherland or faith, Caesar or God. This is the basis of the secularist demand put to Catholics at times that they choose between loyalty to the public school dedicated to producing Americans and loyalty to the parochial school dedicated to producing Catholics. The Christian philosophy of education finds no real antagonism between the two ideals of dedicated citizenry and religious allegiance. They are compatible, one complementing the other.

In the other case, the saving of souls becomes for a minority of well-intentioned people the justification for academic practices and policies that fall far short of what is considered sound and scholarly in the educational world. Happily, this criticism cannot be made of the overwhelming majority of the school systems, but it takes only a few egregious examples to provide ammunition for hostile critics of Catholic education. Especially is this true on the collegiate level.

Perhaps it is an unintentional compliment, for the same strictures are rarely passed with reference to the dozens of second-rate municipal, state, or sectarian colleges springing up everywhere. Nonetheless, the proliferation of Catholic colleges, especially for women, has been the bewilderment of the academic community. Without endowment, without adequately trained faculty, without laboratory facilities and library holdings, without clear academic goals, a number of these institutions have bravely established themselves during the past thirty years, inspired by some vague apostolic mandate. As often as not, the sponsoring group has enjoyed some success in high-school work and so feels thoroughly competent to undertake college work. Sometimes the need to finance the teacher preparation and degree work of their own nuns by opening the doors of the projected college to a few hundred coeds has provided for religious or diocesan superiors an added incentive, over and above the apostolic motive. In any event, they condemn themselves, for the most part, to the limbo of mediocrity; and in the academic marketplace they debase the general coinage of Catholic higher education.

XV

The fourth and perhaps the most serious drawback of the commitment to the elementary school at the Council of Baltimore is the complete reversal of the roles of school and family-Church in the education of the child. This modern phenomenon is a growing source of concern to many bishops and pastors. Too many Catholic families feel absolved of any responsibility for the religious formation of their children once they have entrusted them to the parochial school. "Let the good Sisters take care of it" is not an uncommon attitude. The result has been that on reaching school age, these youngsters are almost totally ignorant of their Catholic faith. In many Catholic homes there is no concerted effort by father or mother to supplement or complement the work of the Catholic school. This situation is far from the ideal of the family and school collaborating in the religious upbringing of the child.

But bad as this situation is, what of the five million

Catholic children for whom there are no Catholic schools? In many instances the parish church is expected to undertake whatever training the boy or girl receives. Here and there, the education program of the Confraternity of Christian Doctrine is doing a thorough job, but hampered by a lack of funds and personnel—the money and teachers are all for the parochial school—the results must fall far short of the promise.

Meanwhile, a probable 75 per cent of the time and energy of the pastor and his assistant is spent on fund-raising devices to keep the parish school afloat. Little time and energy, to say nothing of imagination and initiative, are left over to cope with the dual problem of how to train parents to do their job and how to build an effective religious education program to care for the hundreds of Catholic children in the public schools. In far too many parishes, the school plant dwarfs the church, and school activities seem to dominate parish life completely. What is forgotten is that the center of any parish must be the liturgical life of its people.

XVI

This decade is putting new stresses and strains on both the public school and the Catholic school. These are obviously years of adjustment, both for Catholic education and for public school education. Some of these adjustments will be easier if they are made together. A chapter in the history of American education is closing. Beyond any doubt, striking changes will take place within both school systems and in their relations with one another.

It may not be too much to expect that the recent years of what can at times be called "sunny" dialogue between

Protestants and Catholics are preparing for the day when co-operative ventures, like the shared-time program or a completely overhauled released-time program, will become part of public education.[28] If in the past the subject of religion in education has been an almost constant source of church-state tension and interchurch friction, in the future it may well become a bridge to better understanding.[29]

. . . BY WAY OF BIBLIOGRAPHY

Despite the shelves already heavy with books about American Catholic education, the history remains to be written. Nor should this surprise: we are still awaiting a scholarly one-volume history of the Church itself in this country. The pioneer plowing was done in James A. Burns, *The Principles, Origin and Establishment of the Catholic School System in the United States* (New York, 1908) and *The Growth and Development of the Catholic School System in the United States* (New York, 1912). Bernard Kohlbrenner brought the history forward an-

---

28 "Shared time" is simply a plan to distribute the school hours of the pupil between the state-supported school, which gives general education in a denominationally neutral context, and the church-supported school, which provides certain academic subjects and school activities within its own atmosphere.

29 In a letter to Pope Leo XIII, Cardinal Gibbons explained that the divisions between Catholics and their fellow citizens "are caused above all by the opposition against the system of national education which is attributed to us, and which, more than any other thing, creates and maintains in the minds of the American people the conviction that the Catholic Church is opposed by principle to the institutions of the country, and that a sincere Catholic cannot be a loyal citizen of the United States." Quoted in John Tracy Ellis, *The Life of James Cardinal Gibbons* (Milwaukee, Wis.: The Bruce Publishing Co., 1952), I, 664.

other twenty-five years, while reworking the original Burns volumes, in *A History of Catholic Education in the United States* (New York, 1937).

Francis P. Cassidy sketched the early years of Catholic higher education in *Catholic College Foundations and Development in the United States, 1677–1850* (Washington, D.C., 1924), a work continued by Sebastian A. Erbacher in *Catholic Higher Education for Men in the United States, 1850–1866* (Washington, D.C., 1931). The initial attempt at a comprehensive study of the colleges was Edward J. Power's *A History of Catholic Higher Education in the United States* (Milwaukee, Wis., 1958). Sister M. Mariella Bowler has written *A History of Catholic Colleges for Women in the United States of America* (Washington, D.C., 1933).

Individual colleges which have celebrated fifty, seventy-five, or one hundred and more years have each had their story told, sometimes quite well, more often with an overdose of sentiment. Colman J. Barry has honored his order and himself with *Worship and Work: Saint John's Abbey and University, 1856–1956* (Collegeville, Minn., 1956). Other recent scholarly college histories are John M. Daley's *Georgetown University: Origin and Early Years* (Washington, D.C., 1957) and Wilfred Schoenberg's *Gonzaga University: 75 Years* (Spokane, Wash., 1963).

Again, the older dioceses and teaching groups have usually been celebrated by the local historian. Typical would be Brother Angelus Gabriel's *The Christian Brothers in the United States, 1848–1948* (New York, 1948) and Mary Ellen Evans' *The Spirit Is Mercy: The Story of the Sisters of Mercy in the Archdiocese of Cincinnati, 1858–1958* (Westminster, Md., 1959). Many of these specialized histories are based on excellent doctoral dissertations. Many books in the series out of Catholic University have been valuable contributions, for one instance, Edward M. Connors, *Church-State Relationships in Education in the State of New York* (Washington, D.C., 1951). The masterly three-volume work of Gilbert J. Garraghan, *The Jesuits of the Middle United States* (New York, 1938), is also the finest history of Jesuit education in the Midwest yet written. Several biographies of founders of teaching congregations provide copious material on education. Outstanding in this category is Annabelle Melville, *Elizabeth Bayley Seton, 1774–1821* (New York, 1951).

Naturally, the work of education looms large in the standard histories of the Church. The landmark in the field is the four-volume study of John Gilmary Shea, *The History of the Catholic Church in the United States* (New York, 1886–1892), which brings the Church just past the Civil War. The most useful single-volume work is Theodore Roemer, *The Catholic Church of the United States* (St. Louis, 1951).

Scores of articles have appeared in the leading Catholic periodicals, with many of the best since 1903 reappearing in the *Catholic Mind*. Unhappily, the only cumulative index to this valuable source is in the Mullen Library of Catholic University. Another important guide is the *Woodstock Letters,* since 1872 a kind of Jesuit *Relations* for the New World. A good bibliography of the periodical literature from 1850 to 1950 is Edward R. Vollmar, *The Catholic Church in America: An Historical Bibliography* (New York, 1956).

The author found very helpful several compilations of documents: Peter Guilday, ed., *The National Pastorals of the American Hierarchy, 1792–1919* (Washington, D.C., 1923) and the continuation in Raphael Huber, ed., *Our*

Bishops Speak (Milwaukee, Wis., 1951); John Tracy Ellis, ed., *Documents of American Catholic History* (Milwaukee, Wis., 1956 and 1962); Donald C. Shearer, *Pontificia Americana: A Documentary History of the Catholic Church in the United States, 1784–1884* (Washington, D.C., 1933). The latter work includes all Roman documents dealing directly with the United States. *Education: Papal Teachings* (Boston, 1960) is a translation from the French by the Benedictine monks of Solesmes of the educational pronouncements of the modern popes, beginning with Pius VII. The *Catholic Mind* (New York, 1903–) regularly reprints important addresses and statements on education by the popes and national hierarchies. The most helpful introduction to Catholic sources and published writings is *A Guide to American Catholic History* (Milwaukee, Wis., 1959) by Ellis.

There have been three scholarly biographies of John Carroll, each casting increased light on this gigantic figure: John Gilmary Shea, *Life and Times of the Most Rev. John Carroll, Bishop and First Archbishop of Baltimore* (New York, 1888); Peter Guilday, *The Life and Times of John Carroll, Archbishop of Baltimore, 1735–1815* (New York, 1922); Annabelle M. Melville, *John Carroll of Baltimore: Founder of the American Catholic Hierarchy* (New York, 1955).

The dynamic John Hughes has not yet found his biographer; there is only the outdated John R. Hassard, *Life of the Most Reverend John Hughes, First Archbishop of New York* (New York, 1866). Brownson has fared much better: Henry F. Brownson, *Orestes A. Brownson* (3 vols.; Detroit, 1898–1900); Arthur M. Schlesinger, Jr., *Orestes A. Brownson: A Pilgrim's Progress* Boston, 1939); Theodore Maynard, *Orestes Brownson: Yankee, Radical, Catholic* (New York, 1943). The standard edition of Brownson's writings, *The Works of Orestes A. Brownson* (Detroit, 1882–1907), edited by his son, goes to twenty volumes.

Life of James Cardinal Gibbons, Archbishop of Baltimore (New York, 1922), a two-volume biography by Allen Sinclair Will, has been largely superseded by John Tracy Ellis' two-volume *The Life of James Cardinal Gibbons, Archbishop of Baltimore, 1834–1921* (Milwaukee, Wis., 1952). Patrick H. Ahern's *The Life of John J. Keane, Educator and Archbishop, 1839–1918* (Milwaukee, Wis., 1954) is a careful biography of the first rector of the Catholic University of America, an important contemporary of the cardinal. James A. Moynihan's *The Life of Archbishop John Ireland* (New York, 1953) is worthy of its subject. The St. Paul prelate's collected works are in *The Church and Modern Society: Lectures and Addresses* (2 vols.; St. Paul, Minn., 1904).

The Social Thought of John Lancaster Spalding (Washington, D. C., 1944), by Sister Agnes Claire Schroll, and Monsignor John Tracy Ellis' Gabriel Richard Lecture, *John Lancaster Spalding: First Bishop of Peoria, American Educator* (Milwaukee, Wis., 1961), provide interpretative material on the educational thought of this great bishop. The only complete biography is "The Life of John Lancaster Spalding, First Bishop of Peoria, 1840–1916," an unpublished doctoral dissertation done at Catholic University by David F. Sweeney. Merle Curti devotes a chapter to Spalding in *The Social Ideas of American Educators* (New York, 1935). Of Spalding's numerous writings, the following are especially important: *Means and Ends of Education* (Chicago, 1909); *Religion, Agnosticism and Education* (Chicago, 1902); *Education and the Higher Life* (Chicago, 1891). Frederick J.

Zwierlein produced the monumental three-volume *The Life and Letters of Bishop McQuaid* (Rochester, N.Y., 1925–1927), which is rich in documentation on this important leader.

The pamphlets and tracts of the nineteenth century are unrivaled as source material for the parochial school question and the disputes over religion in the public schools. The Office of Education Library in Washington has the most complete set. Other useful material on the background of the controversies can be found in Sister Mary Augustina, *American Opinion of Roman Catholicism in the Eighteenth Century* (New York, 1936); Ray A. Billington, *The Protestant Crusade, 1800–1860* (New York, 1938); Gustavus Myers, *History of Bigotry in the United States* (New York, 1943). Daniel F. Reilly is the author of *The School Controversy (1891–1893)* (Washington, D.C., 1943). Richard J. Gabel's *Public Funds for Church and Private Schools* (Washington, D.C., 1937) is a mine of information on this subject.

An ocean of ink has gone to write on religion in education, and without a guide one can quickly become marooned amid irrelevance and inanity. Joseph Politella's original compilation, *Religion in Education: An Annotated Bibliography* (Oneonta, N.Y., 1956), has been updated by two other works: Edmond G. Drouin's *The School Question: A Bibliography on Church-State Relationships in American Education, 1940–1960* (Washington D.C., 1963) and John J. McGrath's *Church and State in American Law: Cases and Materials* (Milwaukee, Wis., 1962). The newest addition to this literature is Robert F. Drinan's perceptive *Religion, the Courts, and Public Policy* (New York, 1963). A complete bibliography and specific treatment of the influence of Horace Mann, William T. Harris, and John Dewey in the area of religion and public education may be found in Neil G. McCluskey, *Public Schools and Moral Education* (New York, 1958).

*   *   *

The author wishes to record his appreciation to two friends whose advice and encouragement helped immeasurably in bringing this book into existence: John Tracy Ellis of the Catholic University of America and Frederick G. Hochwalt of the National Catholic Educational Association. His gratitude extends also to the devoted staff of the Mullen Memorial Library of the Catholic University of America, and especially to their genial director, Eugene P. Willging.

Gonzaga University
July 31, 1964

1.   Pastoral Letter of Bishop Carroll*

(1792)

The first bishop of the Catholic Church in the United States was John Carroll, appointed by Pope Pius VII to the pioneer see of Baltimore on November 6, 1789. Two years later, in November, Carroll called the first formal meeting of his priests to discuss the needs of the estimated thirty thousand Catholics scattered throughout the thirteen original states. The following May 28, he published this letter. The first topic broached is education, and about one-third of the pastoral deals with this subject.

John, by Divine permission and with the approbation of the Holy See, Bishop of Baltimore: To my dearly beloved Brethren, the members of the Catholic Church in this Diocess, Health and Blessing, Grace to you and peace from God our Father, and from the Lord Jesus Christ.

The great extent of my diocess and the necessity of ordering many things concerning its government at the beginning of my episcopacy, have not yet permitted me, my dear brethren, to enjoy the consolation, for which I

* Peter Guilday, ed., *The National Pastorals of the American Hierarchy, 1792–1919* (Washington, D.C.: National Catholic Welfare Council, 1923), pp. 2–5.

most earnestly pray, of seeing you all, and of leaving with you, according to the nature of my duty, some words of exhortation, by which you may be strengthened in faith, and encouraged in the exercises of a Christian life. Esteeming myself as a debtor to all, and knowing the rigorous account which I must render for your souls, to the Shepherd of Shepherds, our Lord and Saviour Jesus Christ, I shall have cause to tremble, while I leave anything undone, by which religion and true piety may be promoted, and the means of salvation multiplied for you.

In compliance with the obligation, resulting from the relation in which I stand to you, my endeavours have been turned towards obtaining and applying, for the preservation and extension of faith and for the sanctification of souls, means calculated to produce lasting effects, not only on the present, but on future generations. I thought that Almighty God would make the ministers of His sanctuary, and myself particularly, accountable to Him, if we did not avail ourselves of the liberty enjoyed under our equitable government and just laws, to attempt establishments, in which you, dear brethren, may find permanent resources, suited to your greatest exigencies.

Knowing, therefore, that the principles instilled in the course of a Christian education, are generally preserved through life, and that *a young man according to his way, even when he is old, he will not depart from it* (Proverbs 21:6), I have considered the virtuous and Christian instruction of youth as a principal object of pastoral solicitude. Now who can contribute so much to lighten this burthen, which weighs so heavy on the shoulders of the pastors of souls and who can have so great an interest and special duty in the forming of youthful minds to habits of virtue and religion, as their parents themselves?

Especially while their children retain their native docility, and their hearts are uncorrupted by vice.

How many motives of reason and religion require, that parents should be unwearied in their endeavours, to inspire in them the love and fear of God; docility and submission to His doctrines, and a careful attention to fulfil His commandments? Fathers—bring up your children *in the discipline and correction of the Lord* (Ephesians 6:4). If all, to whom God has given sons and daughters, were assiduous in the discharge of this important obligation, a foundation would be laid for, and great progress made in, the work of establishing a prevailing purity of manners. The same habits of obedience to the will of God; the same principles of a reverential love and fear of Him; and of continual respect for His Holy Name; the same practices of morning and evening prayer; and of the frequentation of the sacraments; the same dread of cursing and swearing; of fraud and duplicity; of lewdness and drunkenness; the same respectful and dutiful behaviour to their fathers and mothers; in a word, the remembrance and influence of the parental counsels and examples received in their youth, would continue with them during life.

And if ever the frailty of nature, or worldly seduction, should cause them to offend God, they would be brought back again to His service and to true repentance by the efficacy of the religious instruction received in their early age. Wherefore, fathers and mothers, be mindful of the words of the Apostles, and bring up your children in the discipline and correction of the Lord. In doing this, you not only render an acceptable service to God, and acquit yourselves of a most important duty, but you labour for the preservation and increase of true religion, for the benefit of our common country, whose welfare depends on the morals of its citizens, and for your own happiness here as well as hereafter; since you may be assured of finding, in those sons and daughters whom you shall train up to virtue and piety, by your instructions and examples, support and consolation in sickness and old age. They will remember with gratitude, and repay with religious duty, your solicitude for them in their infancy and youth.

These being the advantages of a religious education, I was solicitous for the attainment of a blessing so desirable to that precious portion of my flock, the growing generation. A school has been instituted at George-Town, which will continue to be under the superintendence and government of some of my reverend brethren, that is, of men devoted by principle and profession to instruct all, who resort to them, in useful learning, and those of our own religion, in its principles and duties. I earnestly wish, dear brethren, that as many of you, as are able, would send your sons to this school of letters and virtue. I know and lament, that the expense will be too great for many families, and that their children must be deprived of the immediate benefit of this institution; but, indirectly, they will receive it; at least, it may be reasonably expected, that some after being educated at George-Town, and having returned into their own neighbourhood, will become, in their turn, the instructors of the youths who cannot be sent from home; and, by pursuing the same system of uniting much attention to religion with a solicitude for other improvements, the general result will be a great increase of piety, the necessary consequence of a careful instruction in the principles of faith, and Christian morality.

The school, dear brethren, if aided by your benevolence, and favoured with your confidence, will be the foundation of an additional advantage to true religion in this our country. Many amongst us you have experienced inconvenience and disadvantage from the want of spiritual assistance in your greatest necessities, in sickness, in troubles of conscience, and counsels and offices of the ministers of religion. It is notorious to you all, that the present clergymen are insufficient for the exigencies of the faithful; and that they will be more and more so, as the population of our country increases so rapidly; unless, by the providence of our good and merciful God, a constant supply of zealous and able pastors can be formed amongst ourselves; that is, of men accustomed to our climate, and acquainted with the tempers, manners, and government of the people, to whom they are to dispense the ministry of salvation. Now, may we not reasonably hope, that one of the effects of a virtuous course of education will be the preparing of the minds of some, whom providence may select, to receive and cherish a call from God to an ecclesiastical state?

Should such be the designs of infinite mercy on this portion of His flock, all of us, dear brethren, will have new cause to return God thanks for having conducted to our assistance a number of learned and exemplary clergymen, devoted by choice, and formed by experience to the important function of training young Ecclesiastics to all the duties of the ministry. This essential service is already begun by these my respectable brethren. An ecclesiastical seminary, under their immediate direction, and episcopal superintendence, has entered on the important function of raising pastors for your future consolation and improvement; and I cannot forbear recommending their undertaking to your patronage, and what a benefit will they confer on this and future generations, who shall contribute to endow it with some portion of those goods, which themselves have received from a benevolent providence, and for the use of which they must account to Him, from whom they received them?

2. Pastoral Letters
of the Provincial Councils of Baltimore*
(1829–1849)

In 1808, Bishop Carroll requested the Holy See to create four additional dioceses: Bardstown (Kentucky), Boston, New York, and Philadelphia. Rome agreed. Though independent so far as jurisdiction within their own dioceses was concerned, the four (and more as new dioceses continued to be formed) bishops became what are called in the hierarchy of the Church "suffragans" of the Metropolitan See of Baltimore, which was now to be headed by an archbishop. The four dioceses and the archdiocese together made up the Ecclesiastical Province of Baltimore. Seven times between 1829 and 1849 the bishops met in council. On each occasion they informed the faithful of their deliberations and decrees by means of a pastoral. Though the bishops concerned themselves with almost every important aspect of life in the dynamically expanding nation, they returned regularly to certain educational themes. They reminded their listeners of the primacy of the spiritual in the formation of the young. They warned of the moral dangers of the times and of the perils to the faith of the Catholic youngsters in the Protestant-

* Peter Guilday, ed., *The National Pastorals of the American Hierarchy, 1792–1919* (Washington, D.C.: National Catholic Welfare Council, 1923), pp. 24–26; 74; 115–116; 124–125; 133–135; 152–153, 157.

*oriented public schools. Repeatedly, they urged the need
for separate Catholic schools, for sound reading habits,
and for sturdy home life. Vocations to the priesthood and
the religious life as well as the proper training of priests
and teachers were other topics frequently touched upon.
Important excerpts are given here from the five pastorals
more immediately concerned with the schools and formal
education. The letters of 1846 and 1849 are entirely
omitted.*

PASTORAL OF 1829

From this topic [the need for priests] we naturally pass to
that of the education of your children. How important,
how interesting, how awful, how responsible a charge!
"Suffer little children to come unto me, and forbid them
not" says the amiable Jesus, "for of such is the kingdom of
Heaven." Yes! the characteristic of the child, as St. John
Chrysostom well observes, is the characteristic of the
saint. Genuine simplicity without guile, uncalculating
ardent devotion to the loving parent, preferring an
humble mother in her homely garb, to a queen in her
variegated decoration; exercising an irresistible power
over the parental heart by the bewitching confidence of
helplessness itself. Those children, the dear pledges of
your elevated and sanctified affection, deserve and demand your utmost solicitude. For them you brave danger,
on their account you endure toil; you weep over their
afflictions, you rejoice at their gratification, you look forward to their prosperity, you anticipate their gratitude,
your souls are knit to theirs, your happiness is centred
in their good conduct; and you cherish the enlightening
hope that when you and they shall have passed through

this vale of tears, you will be reunited in the kingdom of a common father.

How would your hearts be torn with grief did you foresee, that through eternity those objects of all your best feelings should be cast into outward darkness, where there is weeping and gnashing of teeth! May God in His infinite mercy preserve you and them from the just anticipation of any such result! But, dearly beloved, this is too frequently the necessary consequence of a neglected or an improper education. God has made you the guardians of those children to lead them to His service upon earth, that they might become saints in Heaven. "What will it avail them to gain the whole world if they lose their souls?" Or could it console you in the progress of eternity to recollect that you had for a time beheld them elevated to power, applauded by fame, entrusted with command, swaying nations, dispensing wealth and honours; but misled by vice and now tortured in disgrace; and, thus to be tortured for eternity? If you would avert this dreadful calamity, attend to the education of your child; teaching him first to seek the kingdom of God and His justice, and having food and raiment to be therewith content. Teach him to be industrious, to be frugal, to be humble and fully resigned to the will of that God who feeds the birds of the air, clothes the lily of the field; and who so loved the children of men that when they were His enemies they were reconciled to him by the death of His Son, that being reconciled they might be saved from eternal death by His life being justified now by His blood.

Alas! beloved children, how many are there, who, yielding to the pride of life, and ashamed of Him who was not ashamed for our sakes to die upon an ignominious cross, "being made the reproach of men and the outcast of the people," how many such wretched parents have trained up their children to be themselves the victims of passions in time, and of that death from which there is no resurrection in eternity!

How frequently have their brightest hopes faded away into a settled gloom? How often has the foot which they elevated, spurned them? How often whilst the children of revelry occupied the hall of mirth, has the drink of the wretched parent been mingled with his tears, and whilst his ungrateful offspring, regardless of his admonition, rose in the careless triumph of enjoyment, have his gray hairs been brought with sorrow to the grave? Believe us; it is only by the religious education of your children that you can so train them up, as to ensure that, by their filial piety and their steady virtue, they may be to you the staff of your old age, the source of your consolation, and reward in a better world.

Begin with them in their earliest childhood, whilst the mind is yet pure and docile, and their baptismal innocence uncontaminated; let their unfolding perceptions be imbued with the mild and lovely tints of religious truth and pure devotion; allure them to the service of their creator who delights in the homage of innocence; and give to their reason, as it becomes developed, that substantial nutriment which it requires, and which our holy religion so abundantly affords; shew your children by your conduct, that you believe what you inculcate; natural affection disposes them to imitate your example, you should, therefore, be awfully impressed by that solemn admonition of the Saviour: "Woe to him that shall scandalize one of these little ones that believe in me, it were better for him that a millstone were tied round his neck, and that he were drowned in the depths of the sea."

In placing them at school, seek for those teachers who

will cultivate the seed which you have sown; for of what avail will it be, that you have done so much, if the germs which begin to put forth, shall now be stifled or eradicated; and should tares be sown where you had prepared the soil? Again, and again, would we impress upon your minds the extreme importance of this great duty, and your responsibility to the God of truth, in its regard. How well would it be, if your means and opportunities permitted, were you at this period to commit your children to the care of those whom we have for their special fitness, placed over our seminaries and our female religious institutions? It would be at once the best mode of discharging your obligations to your children, and of aiding us in promoting the great object which we have already endeavoured to impress upon your minds.

Remember also, that not only affection, but, duty requires of you to be vigilant in securing the spiritual concerns of your offspring, during the period of their preparation for business or for professions; that this security can, in general, be far better attained under the parent's roof; or if it be necessary to entrust the sacred deposit of your child's soul to another, it ought to be one of tried virtue, and surrounded by favourable circumstances. Should your family be thus educated, you may naturally expect that they will freely allow your just influence in that most important of all temporal concerns, the selection of a wife or husband; and it becomes you, whilst you pay a proper respect to the affections of those most deeply interested, to be careful that you have more regard to those things which belong to eternity, than to those of a mere transient nature.

.　　.　　.

PASTORAL OF 1833

The education of the rising generation is, beloved brethren, a subject of the first importance; and we have accordingly, at all times, used our best efforts to provide, as far as our means would permit, not only ecclesiastical seminaries to insure a succession in our priesthood and its extension; but we have moreover sought to create colleges and schools in which your children, whether male or female, might have the best opportunities of literature and science, united to a strict protection of their morals and the best safeguards of their faith. You are aware that the success and the permanence of such institutions rest almost exclusively with you. It will be our most gratifying duty to see that their superiors and professors are worthy of the high trust reposed in them; but it is only by your patronage and zealous co-operation that their existence can be secured, their prosperity and usefulness be increased, and your children's children be made to bless the memory, and to pray for the souls of those who originated and upheld such establishments.

.   .   .

PASTORAL OF 1837

We would also beloved brethren, renew the entreaty which we have made to you on other occasions, to unite your efforts to ours for upholding those institutions which we have created for the education of your children. It is our most earnest wish to make them as perfect as possible, in their fitness for the communication and improvement of science, as well as for the cultivation of pure solid and enlightened piety. And if we occasionally experience some difficulty and do not advance as rapidly as the wishes of our friends, or their too sanguine hopes would look for, some allowance must be made for the difficulties by which we are surrounded and the opposition which we experience.

Yet, these notwithstanding, we are persuaded, that amongst those under our superintendence, are to be found, some of the most scientific and literary houses of education which our nation possesses; some establishments for the instruction of youth, male and female, in which there are successfully taught those speculative and practical lessons which inform the understanding, regulate the imagination, cultivate the taste, ameliorate the heart, improve the disposition, impress the importance and obligation of fulfilling every social, civic, domestic and religious duty, and teach the best mode of their performance. And we trust, that by a continuation of that patronage which they have received, we shall be enabled to behold them take deep root in our soul, flourish in beauty and vigour, and furnish an abundant supply of useful citizens and christians, fitted for conferring blessings upon that country which protects them and that religion which they profess.

We would especially commend to your fostering care those pious and meritorious sisterhoods, which in addition to the culture of the youthful mind, gather up the little orphan whom Heaven has deprived of its mother's care, who attend the couch of sickness to moisten the burning lip, to assuage the anguish of pain, to whisper consolation to the raving spirit and to point to the true source of the sinner's hope, when in the dimness of his eye he begins to be sensible of the darkness of the grave.

These are the women, who generously devoting themselves to the whole cause of godlike charity, are found in

good and in evil report; in the school, in the hospital, in
the prison, in the hovel of poverty, in the maniac's cell,
in the midst of pestilence, surrounded by the bodies of
the dying and the corpses of the dead; discharging the
duties of their holy zeal, alike to the professor of their
faith and to its opponent, and tending with the same
assiduity the wretched calumniator of their creed, their
virtue and their sex, as they would their most generous
defender.

.   .   .

PASTORAL OF 1840

There are few subjects dearer to us than the proper education of your children, on this mainly depends their true
respectability in this world, also the consolation of your
own declining years, the prosperity of religion, the honor
of God on earth, and your eternal salvation and that of
your descendants. It is therefore that we have always
deemed it to be one of our most pressing obligations to
use our best and earliest efforts in providing establishments where they may be carefully educated by competent persons in all that is necessary for their prosperity
in this life, whilst they were taught by admonition and
example to walk in that path which leads to heaven. In
general we have found our flocks disposed to profit by
the opportunities thus afforded, but not always so ready
to aid in defraying the expenses which should necessarily
be incurred in having them secured and made permanent.
In many instances also, they who belong not to the household of faith have discovered the advantages which accompanied the system of education in our schools and
colleges; they have often been more industrious to profit

by them than have you, for whom they were principally intended. We would then admonish you, in a spirit of affectionate interest for your own and your children's welfare, that we have in many instances observed two serious mistakes upon this head. The first that of parents, who altogether deprived their offspring of that education to which they were entitled, upon the plea that thereby they would be better served by placing in their hands at their entrance upon a life of industry, the money which had been saved by the restriction of their education. The second that of a mistaken and thriftless economy, which led them to keep their children, especially females, at an inferior school of less cost, until they had nearly gone through those years allotted to education, and then sent them for a comparatively short time to an establishment in which they should have been placed years before.

The great evil in both cases is the danger to which they are exposed, of having their faith undermined, the imperfect instruction which they receive, if they get any, upon the most important subject of religion, the nearly total abandonment of their religious practices and their exposure in their tender youth to the fatal influence of that false shame which generally arises from the mockery or the superciliousness of those who undervalue their creed. Beloved brethren we address you not in the language of speculation or of abstract reasoning; our words are the faint effort to convey to you the deep impression which long and melancholy experience has made upon our minds; for we have witnessed the blastings of our hopes in the ravages which have thus been made.

.   .   .

We are desirous that all under our charge should be as well acquainted with the doctrine found in the Holy

Scriptures as with any other portion of the word of God, we also highly approve of their being familiar with the edifying histories and admirable moral instruction which abound therein, we therefore recommend that the authorised version be found in the houses of the faithful, and that portions of it be frequently read with the veneration which it so well deserves, and meditated upon for the purpose of becoming better acquainted with the providential ways of the Lord, for the amendment of life, for the edification of the well disposed and for the encouragement of virtue.

We desire that at an early period, children should be instructed in the Sacred History, that they may be made acquainted with the nature and value of the divine volume, that they be gradually brought to its perusal with docile hearts, and that in place of allowing them an indiscriminate use of that which is difficult and liable to gross misconstruction, together with what is simple and edifying, they be judiciously led by proper selections, under discreet and pious guides, to the right use of this rich treasure. Moreover, we are disposed to doubt seriously whether the introduction of this sacred volume as an ordinary class book into schools, is beneficial to religion. It is thereby exposed to that irreverend familiarity, which is calculated to produce more contempt than veneration; it is placed side by side with mere human productions, with the fables of mythology and the speculations of a vain philosophy: it is thus too often made the subject of a vulgar jest, it sinks to the level of task-books, and shares the aversion and the remarks which are generally bestowed upon them by children. If the authorised version be used in a school, it should be under circumstances very different from those which are usually found in the public institutions of our States, and this shows the necessity of your better exertions to establish and uphold seminaries and schools, fitted according to our own principles, and for the education of the children who are daily rising up, and numbers of whom are lost for want of such institutions.

There is another evil of which we have still to complain. We can scarcely point out a book in general use in the ordinary schools, or even in higher seminaries, wherein covert and insidious efforts are not made to misrepresent our principles, to distort our tenets, to vilify our practices and to bring contempt upon our Church and its members. The system of which this is a part has been of long standing, and is not peculiar to the United States. It is no easy matter thus to preserve the faith of your children in the midst of so many difficulties. It is not then because of any unkind feeling to our fellow-citizens, it is not through any reluctance on our part, to contribute whatever little we can to the prosperity of what are called the common institutions of the country, that we are always better pleased to have a separate system of education for the children of our communion, but because we have found by a painful experience, that in any common effort it was always expected that our distinctive principles of religious belief and practice should be yielded to the demands of those who thought proper to charge us with error; and because we saw with great pain the differences which an attempt to combine and to conciliate principles, which we have never been able to reconcile, has produced in a distant Church which has always been found faithful.

We are happy to perceive the existence of a spirit to sustain the efforts recently made to supply our schools, and our families with some books, which whilst they remove the discolourings of fiction, and vindicate the truth of history, will rescue from unmerited censure a portion of our illustrious dead, without doing violence to the feelings of even our opponents. We are anxious that truth and charity should have dominion in every place, but especially in our schools. We should be gratified to behold the books of earlier instruction also prepared upon the same principle, and we strenuously recommend to you to encourage and to sustain those who, being properly qualified, may undertake the task.

It is but a few years since the schools, which the female religious orders and congregations so usefully superintend, were extensively spread abroad through our Union; already you have gathered rich fruits from the exertions of those virtuous and laborious sisters. The peculiar blessing of heaven appears to rest upon their work, calumny has failed in her vile efforts to taint their fair fame: popular frenzy has been excited by every bad art to effect their ruin, but with one notorious exception, it has been restrained and rebuked, and now we may feel confident, under the blessing of heaven, that in a short period, under your auspices our female children will have secured to them, whether they be blessed with the goods of this world or tried by poverty, the mighty boon of as perfect a system of education as need be admired; nor shall we be subject to the partizan spirit of political leaders, nor dependent upon the unsteady and contested votes of legislative halls for its continuance.

Respecting our colleges and schools for males, though much has been effected, yet much remains to be done by their multiplication, and we exhort you for the sake of your children, your country and your religion, to come to our aid for the purpose of making the effort thus to provide for the literary, moral and religious education of one sex as well as of the other. We have exposed to you the danger of their position, we confide in your charity and in your zeal.

PASTORAL OF 1843

The transmission of faith to their children was a special object of the solicitude of our fathers: for which they thought no sacrifice too great. It must be your care, brethren, to let the precious inheritance descend without diminution. You must, therefore, use all diligence that your children be instructed at an early age in the saving truths of religion, and be preserved from the contagion of error. We have seen with serious alarm, efforts made to poison the fountains of public education, by giving it a sectarian hue, and accustoming children to the use of a version of the Bible made under sectarian bias, and placing in their hands books of various kinds replete with offensive and dangerous matter. This is plainly opposed to the free genius of our civil institutions. We admonish parents of the awful account they must give at the divine tribunal, should their children, by their neglect or connivance, be imbued with false principles, and led away from the path of salvation. Parents are strictly bound, like faithful Abraham, to teach their children the truths which God has revealed; and if they suffer them to be led astray, the souls of the children will be required at their hands. Let them, therefore, avail themselves of their natural rights, guaranteed by the laws, and see that no interference with the faith of their children be used in the public schools, and no attempt made to induce conformity in any thing contrary to the laws of the Catholic Church. . . .

We cannot withhold the expression of our consolation at the success which has crowned the apostolic labors of missionaries of the Society of Jesus in the vast regions occupied by Indian tribes, especially in the Oregon territory west of the Rocky Mountains. With zeal worthy of the brightest ages of the Church, they have gone to those children of nature to civilize them, and impart to them the knowledge of salvation, and God has confirmed their word, and made it fruitful.

3. Petition of the Catholics of New York for a Portion of the Common-School Fund* (1840)

The scene of the first significant struggle by Catholics to obtain a proportionate share of the common-school fund was New York City. Between 1795 and 1825, all the city's schools, most of which were under church sponsorship, had received direct financial support from state funds. In 1805, the Free School Society was founded "for the education of such poor children as do not belong to, or are not provided for by any religious society." A few years later, it adopted the name "Public School Society" and rapidly became the most powerful educational organization in New York. In 1824, the legislature gave the Board of Aldermen authority to select the institutions eligible for state funds. From 1825 on, New York City's share of the state school fund was given exclusively to the nonsectarian Public School Society, except for minor grants to orphanages and mission schools. The issue rose stormily again in 1840, when Governor William H. Seward publicly proposed that state money be used to establish schools under church auspices for immigrant children. The inspiration behind the petition was Arch-

* *Complete Works of the Most Rev. John Hughes* (New York: Lawrence Kehoe, 1866), I, 102–107.

*bishop John Hughes, who labored tirelessly but in vain
to sell the case for the Catholic school to his fellow
citizens.*

TO THE HONORABLE THE BOARD OF
ALDERMEN OF THE CITY OF NEW YORK

*The Petition of the Catholics of New York,
Respectfully represents:*

That your Petitioners yield to no class in their performance of, and disposition to perform all the duties of
citizens.—They bear, and are willing to bear, their portion of every common burden; and feel themselves entitled to a participation in every common benefit.

This participation, they regret to say, has been denied
them for years back, in reference to Common School Education in the city of New York, except on conditions with
which their conscience, and, as they believe their duty
to God, did not, and do not leave them at liberty to
comply.

The rights of conscience, in this country, are held by
the constitution and universal consent to be sacred and
inviolate. No stronger evidence of this need be adduced
than the fact, that one class of citizens are exempted from
the duty or obligation of defending their country against
an invading foe, out of delicacy and deference to the
rights of conscience which forbids them to take up arms
for any purpose.

Your Petitioners only claim the benefit of this principle in regard to the public education of their children.
They regard the public education which the State has
provided as a common benefit, in which they are most

desirous and feel that they are entitled to participate; and therefore they pray your Honorable Body that they may be permitted to do so, without violating their conscience.

But your Petitioners do not ask that this prayer be granted without assigning their reasons for preferring it.

In ordinary cases men are not required to assign the motives of conscientious scruples in matters of this kind. But your petitioners are aware that a large, wealthy and concentrated influence is directed against their claim by the Corporation called the Public School Society. And that this influence, acting on a public opinion already but too much predisposed to judge unfavorably of the claims of your petitioners, requires to be met by facts which justify them in thus appealing to your Honorable Body, and which may, at the same time, convey a more correct impression to the public mind. Your petitioners adopt this course the more willingly, because the justice and impartiality which distinguish the decisions of public men, in this country, inspire them with the confidence that your Honorable Body will maintain, in their regard, the principle of the rights of conscience, if it can be done without violating the rights of others, and on no other condition is the claim solicited.

It is not deemed necessary to trouble your Honorable Body with a detail of the circumstances by which the monopoly of the public education of children in the city of New York, and of the funds provided for that purpose at the expense of the State, have passed into the hands of a private corporation, styled in its Act of Charter, "The Public School Society of the City of New York." It is composed of men of different sects or denominations. But that denomination, Friends, which is believed to have the controlling influence, both by its numbers and otherwise, holds as a peculiar *sectarian principle* that any formal or official teaching of religion is, at best, unprofitable. And your petitioners have discovered that such of *their* children as have attended the public schools, are generally, and at an early age, imbued with the same principle—that they become untractable, disobedient, and even contemptuous towards their parents—unwilling to learn any thing of religion—as if they had become illuminated, and could receive all the knowledge of religion necessary for them by instinct or inspiration. Your petitioners do not pretend to assign the cause of this change in their children, they only attest the fact, as resulting from their attendance at the public schools of the Public School Society.

This Society, however, is composed of gentlemen of various sects, including even one or two Catholics. But they profess to exclude all sectarianism from their schools. If they do not exclude sectarianism, they are avowedly no more entitled to the school funds than your petitioners, or any other denomination of professing Christians. If they do, as they profess, exclude sectarianism, then your petitioners contend that they exclude Christianity—and leave to the advantage of infidelity the tendencies which are given to the minds of youth by the influence of this feature and pretension of their system.

If they could accomplish what they profess, other denominations would join your petitioners in remonstrating against their schools. But they do not accomplish it. Your petitioners will show your Honorable Body that they do admit what Catholics call sectarianism, (although others may call it only religion,) in a great variety of ways.

In their 22d report, as far back as the year 1827, they tell us, page 14, that they *"are aware of the importance* of early RELIGIOUS INSTRUCTION," and that none but what is *"exclusively general and scriptural in its character should be introduced into the schools under their charge."* Here, then, is their own testimony that they did introduce and authorize "religious instruction" in their schools. And that they solved, with the utmost composure, the difficult question on which the sects disagree, by determining *what kind* of *"religious instruction"* is *"exclusively general and scriptural in its character."* Neither could they impart this "early religious instruction" themselves. They must have left it to their teachers—and these, armed with official influence, could impress those "early religious instructions" on the susceptible minds of the children, with the authority of dictators.

The Public School Society, in their report for the year 1832, page 10, describe the effect of these "early religious instructions," without, perhaps, intending to do so; but yet precisely as your petitioners have witnessed it, in such of their children as attended those schools. *"The age at which children are usually sent to school affords a much better opportunity to mould their minds to peculiar and exclusive forms of faith than any subsequent period of life."* In page 11, of the same report, they protest against the injustice of supporting "religion in any shape" by public money; as if the "early religious instruction" which they had themselves authorized in their schools, five years before, was not "religion in some shape," and was not supported by public taxation. They tell us again, in more guarded language, "The Trustees are deeply impressed with the importance of imbuing the youthful mind with religious impressions, and they have endeavored to attain this object, as far as the nature of the institution will admit." Report of 1837.

In their Annual Report they tell us, that "they would not be understood as regarding religious impressions in early youth as unimportant; on the contrary, they desire to do all which may with propriety be done, to give a right direction to the minds of the children intrusted to their care. Their schools are uniformly opened with the reading of the Scriptures, and the class-books are such as recognize and enforce the great and generally acknowledged principles of Christianity." Page 7.

In their 34th Annual Report, for the year 1839, they pay a high compliment to a deceased teacher for "the moral and religious influence exerted by her over the three hundred girls daily attending her school," and tell us that it could not but have had a lasting effect on many of their "susceptible minds." Page 7. And yet in all these "early religious instructions, religious impressions, and religious influence," essentially anti-Catholic, your petitioners are to see nothing sectarian; but if in giving the education which the State requires, they were to bring the same influences to bear on the "susceptible minds" of their *own* children, in favor, and not against, their *own* religion, then this society contends that it would be sectarian!

Your petitioners regret that there is no means of ascertaining to what extent the teachers in the schools of this Society carried out the views of their principals on the importance of conveying "early religious instructions" to the "susceptible minds" of their children. But they believe it is in their power to prove, that in some instances, the Scriptures have been explained, as well as read to the pupils.

Even the reading of the Scriptures in those schools your petitioners cannot regard otherwise than as sectarian; because Protestants would certainly consider as such the

introduction of the Catholic Scriptures, which are different from theirs, and the Catholics have the same ground
of objection when the Protestant version is made use of.

Your petitioners have to state further, as grounds of
their conscientious objections to those schools, that many
of the selections in their elementary reading lessons contain matter prejudicial to the Catholic name and character.* The term "Popery" is repeatedly found in them.
This term is known and employed as one of insult and
contempt towards the Catholic religion, and it passes into
the minds of children with the feeling of which it is the
outward expression. Both the historical and religious
portions of the reading lessons are selected from Protestant writers, whose prejudices against the Catholic religion render them unworthy of confidence in the mind
of your petitioners, at least so far as their own children
are concerned.

The Public School Society have heretofore denied that
their books contained any thing reasonably objectionable
to Catholics. Proofs of the contrary could be multiplied,
but it is unnecessary, as they have recently retracted their
denial, and discovered, after fifteen years' enjoyment of
their monopoly, that their books do contain objectionable

---

* The Catholic complaint was well-grounded. Here is a sample
cited by Archbishop Hughes: "As for old Phelim Maghee, he was of
no particular religion. When Phelim had laid up a good stock of
sins, he now and then went over to Killarney, of a Sabbath morning,
and got *relaaf* by *confissing* them out o' the way, as he used to express it, and sealed his soul up with a *wafer*, and returned quite
invigorated for the perpetration of new offences." And another:
"That religion is most likely to find professors among the frivolous
and the wicked, which by a species of ecclesiastical legerdemain can
persuade the sinner that he is going to heaven when he is going
directly to hell. By a refined and complicated system of Jesuitry and
prelatical juggling, the papal see has obtained its present extensive
influence through the world." Quoted in *Complete Works*, I, 52–53.
—N. G. McC.

passages. But they allege that they have proffered repeatedly to make such corrections as the Catholic Clergy
might require. Your petitioners conceive that such a
proposal could not be carried into effect by the Public
School Society without giving just ground for exception
to other denominations. Neither can they see with what
consistency that Society can insist, as it has done, on the
perpetuation of its monopoly, when the Trustees thus
avow their incompetency to present unexceptionable
books, without the aid of the Catholic, or any other
Clergy. They allege, indeed, that with the best intentions
they have been unable to ascertain the passages which
might be offensive to Catholics. With their intentions,
your petitioners cannot enter into any question. Nevertheless, they submit to your Honorable Body, that this
Society is eminently incompetent to the superintendence
of public education, if they could not see that the following passage was unfit for the public schools, and especially unfit to be placed in the hands of Catholic children.

They will quote the passage as one instance, taken from
Putnam's Sequel, page 266:

"HUSS, JOHN, *a zealous reformer from Popery, who
lived in Bohemia, towards the close of the fourteenth,
and beginning of the fifteenth centuries. He was bold and
persevering; but at length, trusting himself to the deceit-
ful Catholics, he was by them brought to trial, condemned as a heretic, and burnt at the stake.*"

The Public School Society may be excused for not
knowing the historical inaccuracies of this passage; but
surely assistance of the Catholic Clergy could not have
been necessary to an understanding of the word "de-
ceitful," as applied to all who profess the religion of
your petitioners.

For these reasons, and others of the same kind, your

VERNON REGIONAL
JUNIOR COLLEGE LIBRARY

petitioners cannot, in conscience, and consistently with their sense of duty to God, and to their offspring, intrust the Public School Society with the office of giving "a right direction to the minds of their children." And yet this Society claims that office, and claims for the discharge of it the Common School Funds, to which your petitioners, in common with other citizens, are contributors. In so far as they are contributors, they are not only deprived of any benefit in return, but their money is employed to the damage and detriment of their religion, in the minds of their own children, and of the rising generation of the community at large. The contest is between the *guarantied* rights, civil and religious, of the citizen on the one hand, and the pretensions of the Public School Society on the other; and whilst it has been silently going on for years, your petitioners would call the attention of your Honorable Body to its consequences on that class for whom the benefits of public education are most essential—the children of the poor.

This class (your petitioners speak only so far as relates to their own denomination), after a brief experience of the schools of the Public School Society, naturally and deservedly withdrew all confidence from it. Hence the establishment by your petitioners of schools for the education of the poor. The expense necessary for this, was a second taxation, required not by the laws of the land, but by the no less imperious demands of their conscience.

They were reduced to the alternative of seeing their children growing up in entire ignorance, or else taxing themselves anew for private schools, whilst the funds provided for education, and contributed in part by themselves, were given over to the Public School Society, and by them employed as has been stated above.

Now your petitioners respectfully submit, that without

this confidence, no body of men can discharge the duties of education as intended by the State, and required by the people. The Public School Society are, and have been at all times, conscious that they had not the confidence of the poor. In their twenty-eighth report, they appeal to the ladies of New York to create or procure it, by the "persuasive eloquence of female kindness;" page 5. And from this they pass, on the next page, to the more efficient eloquence of coercion under penalties and privations to be visited on all persons, "whether emigrants or otherwise," who being in the circumstances of poverty referred to, should not send their children to some "public or other daily school." In their twenty-seventh report, pages 15 and 16, they plead for the doctrine, and recommend it to public favor by the circumstance that it will affect but "few natives." But why should it be necessary at all, if they possessed that confidence of the poor, without which they need never hope to succeed? So well are they convinced of this, that no longer ago than last year, they gave up all hope of inspiring it, and loudly call for coercion by *"the strong arm of the civil power"* to supply its deficiency. Your petitioners will close this part of their statement with the expression of their surprise and regret that gentlemen who are themselves indebted much to the respect which is properly cherished for the rights of conscience, should be so unmindful of the same rights in the case of your petitioners. Many of them are by religious principle so pacific that they would not take up arms in the defence of the liberties of their country, though she should call them to her aid; and yet, they do not hesitate to invoke the "strong arm of the civil power" for the purpose of abridging the private liberties of their fellow-citizens, who may feel equally conscientious.

Your petitioners have to deplore, as a consequence of

this state of things, the ignorance and vice to which hundreds, nay thousands of their children are exposed. They have to regret, also, that the education which they can provide, under the disadvantages to which they have been subjected, is not as efficient as it should be. But should your Honorable Body be pleased to designate their schools as entitled to receive a just proportion of the public funds which belong to your petitioners in common with other citizens, their schools could be improved for those who attend, others now growing up in ignorance could be received, and the ends of the Legislature could be accomplished—a result which is manifestly hopeless under the present system.

Your petitioners will now invite the attention of your Honorable Body to the objections and misrepresentations that have been urged by the Public School Society to granting the claim of your petitioners. It is urged by them that it would be appropriating money raised by general taxation to the support of the Catholic religion. Your petitioners join issue with them, and declare unhesitatingly, that if this objection can be established the claim shall be forthwith abandoned. It is objected that though we are taxed as citizens, we apply for the benefits of education as "Catholics." Your petitioners, to remove this difficulty, beg to be considered in their application in the identical capacity in which they are taxed—viz.: as citizens of the commonwealth. It has been contended by the Public School Society, that the law disqualifies schools which admit any profession of religion, from receiving any encouragements from the School Fund. Your petitioners have two solutions for this pretended difficulty. 1. Your petitioners are unable to discover any such disqualification in the law, which merely delegates to your Honorable Body the authority and discretion of determining what schools or societies shall be entitled to its bounty. 2. Your petitioners are willing to fulfill the conditions of the law so far as religious teaching is proscribed during school hours. In fine, your petitioners, to remove all objections, are willing that the material organization of their schools, and the disbursements of the funds allowed for them, shall be conducted, and made, by persons unconnected with the religion of your petitioners, even the Public School Society, if it should please your Honorable Body to appoint them for that purpose. The public may then be assured that the money will not be applied to the support of the Catholic religion.

It is deemed necessary by your petitioners to save the Public School Society the necessity of future misconception, thus to state the things which are *not* petitioned for. The members of that Society, who have shown themselves so impressed with the importance of conveying *their* notions of "early religious instruction" to the "susceptible minds" of Catholic children, can have no objection that the parents of the children, and teachers in whom the parents have confidence, should do the same, provided no law is violated thereby, and no disposition evinced to bring the children of other denominations within its influence.

Your petitioners, therefore, pray that your Honorable Body will be pleased to designate, as among the schools entitled to participate in the Common School Fund, upon complying with the requirements of the law, and the ordinances of the corporation of the city—or for such other relief as to your Honorable Body shall seem meet— St. Patrick's School, St. Peter's School, St. Mary's School, St. Joseph's School, St. James' School, St. Nicholas' School, Transfiguration Church School, and St. John's School.

And your petitioners further request, in the event of

your Honorable Body's determining to hear your petitioners, on the subject of their petition, that such time may be appointed as may be most agreeable to your Honorable Body, and that a full session of your Honorable Board be convened for that purpose.

And your petitioners, &c.

THOMAS O'CONNOR, *Chairman.*

GREGORY DILLON, ANDREW CARRIGAN, PETER DUFFY, *Vice-Chairmen.*

Of a general meeting of the Catholics of the City of New York, convened in the schoolroom of St. James' Church, Sept. 21, 1840.

B. O'CONNER, JAMES KELLY, J. M'LOUGHLIN, *Secretaries.*

4. The Plenary Councils of Baltimore

First Plenary Council* (1852)

Vast expansion occurred within the Catholic Church during the middle decades of the nineteenth century. From the original Ecclesiastical Province of Baltimore, which was coextensive with the limits of the United States itself, were formed the Province of Oregon City (1846) and the Province of St. Louis (1847). By the opening of the 1852 council, Rome had erected three more ecclesiastical provinces: New Orleans, Cincinnati, and New York. To this gathering, which now took on a national or plenary nature, came the six archbishops and thirty-five suffragan bishops of the country. Their pastoral treats mainly of church authority and Catholic education.

No portion of our charge fills us with greater solicitude than that which our Divine Master, by word and example, has taught us to regard with more than ordinary sentiments of affection—the younger members of our flock. If our youth grow up in ignorance of their religious duties or unpractised in their consoling fulfilment; if, instead of the words of eternal life, which find so full

* Peter Guilday, ed., *The National Pastorals of the American Hierarchy, 1792–1919* (Washington, D.C.: National Catholic Welfare Council, 1923), pp. 189–191.

and sweet an echo in the heart of innocence, the principles of error, unbelief or indifferentism, are imparted to them; if the natural repugnance, even in the happiest period of life, to bend under the yoke of discipline, be increased by the example of those whose relation to them gives them influence or authority,—what are we to expect but the disappointment of all hopes which cause the Church to rejoice in the multiplication of her children!

We therefore address you brethren, in the language of affectionate warning and solemn exhortation. Guard carefully those little ones of Christ; "suffer them to approach Him, and prevent them not, for of such is the kingdom of heaven." To you, Christian parents, God has committed these His children, whom He permits you to regard as yours; and your natural affection towards whom must ever be subordinate to the will of Him "from whom all paternity in heaven and on earth is named." Remember that if for them you are the representatives of God, the source of their existence, you are to be for them depositaries of His authority, teachers of His law, and models by imitating which they may be perfect, even as their Father in heaven is perfect.

You are to watch over the purity of their faith and morals with jealous vigilance, and to instil into their young hearts principles of virtue and perfection. What shall be the anguish of the parent's heart,—what terrible expectation of judgment that will fill his soul, should his children perish through his criminal neglect, or his obstinate refusal to be guided in the discharge of his paternal duties, by the authority of God's Church. To avert this evil give your children a Christian education, that is an education based on religious principles, accompanied by religious practices and always subordinate to religious influence. Be not led astray by the false and delusive theories which are so prevalent, and which leave youth without religion, and, consequently, without anything to control the passions, promote the real happiness of the individual, and make society find in the increase of its members, a source of security and prosperity. Listen not to those who would persuade you that religion can be separated from secular instruction.

If your children, while they advance in human sciences, are not taught the science of the saints, their minds will be filled with every error, their hearts will be receptacles of every vice, and that very learning which they have acquired, in itself so good and so necessary, deprived of all that could shed on it the light of heaven, will be an additional means of destroying the happiness of the child, embittering still more the chalice of parental disappointment, and weakening the foundations of social order.

Listen to our voice, which tells you to walk in the ancient paths; to bring up your children as you yourselves were brought up by your pious parents; to make religion the foundation of the happiness you wish to secure for those whom you love so tenderly, and the promotion of whose interests is the motive of all your efforts, the solace which sustains you in all your fatigues and privations.

Encourage the establishment and support of Catholic schools; make every sacrifice which may be necessary for this object: spare our hearts the pain of beholding the youth whom, after the example of our Master, we so much love, involved in all the evils of an uncatholic education, evils too multiplied and too obvious to require that we should do more than raise our voices in solemn protest against the system from which they spring.

In urging on you the discharge of this duty, we are acting on the suggestion of the Sovereign Pontiff, who in an encyclical letter, dated 21 November, 1851, calls on all the Bishops of the Catholic world, to provide for the religious education of youth. We are following the example of the Irish Hierarchy, who are courageously opposing the introduction of a system based on the principle which we condemn, and who are now endeavoring to unite religious with secular instruction of the highest order, by the institution of a Catholic University,—an undertaking in the success of which we necessarily feel a deep interest, and which, as having been suggested by the Sovereign Pontiff, powerfully appeals to the sympathies of the whole Catholic world.

Second Plenary Council* (1866)

The saddest chapter in America's history was written in blood between the First and Second Plenary Councils. Within a year of the peace that came at Appomattox to end the Civil War, Archbishop Martin J. Spalding of Baltimore received permission from Rome to call a national council so, as he phrased it in a letter of summons, "that at the close of the national crisis, which had acted as a dissolvent upon all sectarian ecclesiastical institutions, the Catholic Church might present to the country and the world a striking proof of the strong bond of unity with which her members are knit together." Two chapters of the resulting pastoral are printed here.

EDUCATION OF YOUTH

We recur to the subject of the education of youth, to which, in the former Plenary Council, we already directed your attention, for the purpose of reiterating the admonition we then gave, in regard to the establishment and support of Parochial Schools; and of renewing the expression of our conviction, that religious teaching and religious training should form part of every system of school education.

* Peter Guilday, ed., *The National Pastorals of the American Hierarchy, 1792–1919* (Washington, D.C.: National Catholic Welfare Council, 1923), pp. 215–217.

Every day's experience renders it evident, that to develop the intellect and store it with knowledge, while the heart and its affections are left without the control of religious principle, sustained by religious practices, is to mistake the nature and object of education; as well as to prepare for parent and child the most bitter disappointment in the future, and for society the most disastrous results.

We wish also to call attention to a prevalent error on the subject of the education of youth, from which parents of the best principles are not always exempt. Naturally desiring the advancement of their children, in determining the education they will give them, they not unfrequently consult their wishes, rather than their means, and the probable position of their children in mature age. Education, to be good, need not necessarily be either high or ornamental, in the studies or accomplishments it embraces. These things are in themselves unobjectionable; and they may be suitable and advantageous or otherwise, according to circumstances.

Prepare your children for the duties of the state or condition of life they are likely to be engaged in: do not exhaust your means in bestowing on them an education that may unfit them for these duties. This would be a sure source of disappointment and dissatisfaction, both for yourselves and for them. Accustom them from their earliest years to habits of obedience, industry, and thrift: and deeply impress on their minds the great principle, that happiness and success in life, as well as acceptance with God, do not so much depend on the station we fill, as on the fidelity with which we discharge its duties. Teach them, that the groundwork of true happiness must be placed in habitual and cheerful submission of our wills to the dispensations of Providence, who has

wisely consulted for the happiness of all, without, however, bestowing on all an equal share of the goods of
fortune.

CATHOLIC PROTECTORIES
AND INDUSTRIAL SCHOOLS

Connected with this subject of education, is the establishment of Protectories and Industrial Schools for the
correction or proper training of youth, which has of late
years attracted universal attention. It is a melancholy
fact, and a very humiliating avowal for us to make, that
a very large proportion of the idle and vicious youth of
our principal cities are the children of Catholic parents.
Whether from poverty or neglect, the ignorance in
which so many parents are involved as to the true nature
of education, and of their duties as Christian parents, or
the associations which our youth so easily form with
those who encourage them to disregard parental admonition; certain it is, that a large number of Catholic
parents either appear to have no idea of the sanctity
of the Christian family, and of the responsibility imposed
on them of providing for the moral training of their offspring, or fulfil this duty in a very imperfect manner.

Day after day, these unhappy children are caught in
the commission of petty crimes, which render them
amenable to the public authorities; and, day after day,
are they transferred by hundreds from the sectarian
reformatories in which they have been placed by the
courts, to distant localities, where they are brought up
in ignorance of, and most commonly in hostility to, the
Religion in which they had been baptized. The only
remedy for this great and daily augmenting evil is, to

provide Catholic Protectories or Industrial Schools, to which such children may be sent; and where, under the only influence that is known to have really reached the roots of vice, the youthful culprit may cease to do evil and learn to do good.

We rejoice that in some of our dioceses—would that we could say in all!—a beginning has been made in this good work; and we cannot too earnestly exhort our Venerable Brethren of the Clergy to bring this matter before their respective flocks, to endeavor to impress on Christian parents the duty of guarding their children from the evils above referred to, and to invite them to make persevering and effectual efforts for the establishment of Institutions, wherein, under the influence of religious teachers, the waywardness of youth may be corrected, and good seed planted in the soil in which, while men slept, the enemy had sowed tares.

Third Plenary Council* (1884)

For upward of four decades, the Catholic community of the United States had tried to come to terms with the Protestant majority on the school situation. Catholics had attempted without success to obtain a share of the school-tax moneys to put up their own schools. Lacking the material resources to provide parish schools in sufficient numbers, the predominantly immigrant and working-class Catholic group had little choice but to put their youngsters into the public schools where, from a Catholic point of view, the religious atmosphere was often intolerable. Leakage from the Church was serious.† Hundreds of thousands of Catholic children were growing up in almost complete ignorance of their heritage of faith. Schools were very much on everyone's mind when the

* *Acta et decreta concilii plenarii Baltimorensis tertii* (Baltimore: John Murphy & Co., 1886): English text of the pastoral letter, pp. lxxviii–lxxix, lxxxii–lxxxvi; Latin text of the decrees, p. 104.

† A Presbyterian minister was quoted by Bishop Bernard J. McQuaid of Rochester as openly avowing "that the Bible and the Common Schools were two stones of the mill that would grind Catholicity out of Catholics," and a Methodist minister, as boasting that in twelve years, the Catholics had lost 1,900,000 children. Cited in Richard J. Gabel, *Public Funds for Church and Private Schools* (Washington, D.C.: The Catholic University of America Press, 1937), p. 487. Were parents failing? Obviously to some extent. It must be remembered, however, that the immigrant was probably illiterate himself, that he generally worked a twelve- to fourteen-hour day and a six-day week, that often a language barrier grew up between him and his child in school. Perhaps the real wonder is that so many did manage to keep the faith.

*fourteen archbishops and sixty bishops of the country
assembled in 1884 for the last and greatest of the national
councils.* Following the excerpts from the pastoral are
two of the critical decrees passed by the bishops.†*

One of our first cares has been to provide for the more
perfect education of aspirants to the holy Priesthood. It
has always been the Church's endeavor that her clergy
should be eminent in learning. For she has always considered that nothing less than this is required by their
sacred office of guarding and dispensing Divine truth.
"The lips of the priest shall keep knowledge," says the
Most High, "and the people shall seek the law at his
mouth" (Malachy 2:7). This is true in all times; for no
advance in secular knowledge, no diffusion of popular
education, can do away with the office of the teaching
ministry, which Our Lord has declared shall last forever. In every age it is and shall be the duty of God's
priests to proclaim the salutary truths which our Heav-
enly Father has given to each generation in the way
that will move their minds and hearts to embrace and
love them; to defend them, when necessary, against
every attack of error. From this it is obvious that the
priest should have a wide acquaintance with every department of learning that has a bearing on religious
truth. Hence in our age, when so many misleading
theories are put forth on every side, when every de-

---

* Why were there no later councils? By 1884, sufficient uniformity
on matters of discipline had been achieved, and this had been the
principal objective of the gatherings. The more than two hundred
bishops of today's 147 dioceses do, in fact, hold a week-long meeting
each year to discuss common problems.

† The attitude of the council toward education was strongly
affected by the Instruction sent from Rome in 1875 (see pp. 121–126).

partment of natural truth and fact is actively explored for objections against revealed religion, it is evident how extensive and thorough should be the knowledge of the minister of the Divine Word, that he may be able to show forth worthily the beauty, the superiority, the necessity of the Christian religion, and to prove that there is nothing in all that God has made to contradict anything that God has taught.

Hence the priest who has the noble ambition of attaining to the high level of his holy office, may well consider himself a student all his life; and of the leisure hours which he can find amid the duties of his ministry, he will have very few that he can spare for miscellaneous reading, and none at all to waste. And hence, too, the evident duty devolving on us, to see that the course of education in our ecclesiastical colleges and seminaries be as perfect as it can be made.

Scarcely, if at all, secondary to the Church's desire for the education of the clergy, is her solicitude for the education of the laity. It is not for themselves, but for the people, that the Church wishes her clergy to be learned, as it is not for themselves only, but for the people that they are priests. Popular education has always been a chief object of the Church's care; in fact, it is not too much to say that the history of civilization and education is the history of the Church's work. In the rude ages, when semibarbarous chieftains boasted of their illiteracy, she succeeded in diffusing that love of learning which covered Europe with schools and universities; and thus from the barbarous tribes of the early middle ages, she built up the civilized nations of modern times. Even subsequent to the religious dissensions of the sixteenth century, whatever progress has been made in education is mainly due to the impetus which she had previously given. In our own country notwithstanding the many difficulties attendant on first beginnings and unexampled growth, we already find her schools, academies and colleges everywhere, built and sustained by voluntary contributions, even at the cost of great sacrifices, and comparing favorably with the best educational institutions in the land.

These facts abundantly attest the Church's desire for popular instruction. The beauty of truth, the refining and elevating influences of knowledge, are meant for all, and she wishes them to be brought within the reach of all. Knowledge enlarges our capacity both for self-improvement and for promoting the welfare of our fellow-men; and in so noble a work the Church wishes every hand to be busy. Knowledge, too, is the best weapon against pernicious errors. It is only "a little learning" that is "a dangerous thing." In days like ours, when error is so pretentious and aggressive, every one needs to be as completely armed as possible with sound knowledge,—not only the clergy, but the people also that they may be able to withstand the noxious influences of popularized irreligion.

In the great coming combat between truth and error, between Faith and Agnosticism, an important part of the fray must be borne by the laity, and woe to them if they are not well prepared. And if, in the olden days of vassalage and serfdom, the Church honored every individual, no matter how humble his position, and labored to give him the enlightenment that would qualify him for future responsibilities, much more now, in the era of popular rights and liberties, when every individual is an active and influential factor in the body politic, does she desire that all should be fitted by suitable training for an intelligent and conscientious discharge of the important duties that will devolve upon them.

Few, if any, will deny that a sound civilization must depend upon sound popular education. But education, in order to be sound and to produce beneficial results, must develop what is best in man, and make him not only clever but good. A one-sided education will develop a one-sided life; and such a life will surely topple over, and so will every social system that is built up of such lives. True civilization requires that not only the physical and intellectual, but also the moral and religious, well-being of the people should be promoted, and at least with equal care. Take away religion from a people, and morality would soon follow; morality gone, even their physical condition will ere long degenerate into corruption which breeds decrepitude, while their intellectual attainments would only serve as a light to guide them to deeper depths of vice and ruin. This has been so often demonstrated in the history of the past, and is, in fact, so self-evident, that one is amazed to find any difference of opinion about it. A civilization without religion, would be a civilization of "the struggle for existence, and the survival of the fittest," in which cunning and strength would become the substitutes for principle, virtue, conscience and duty. As a matter of fact, there never has been a civilization worthy of the name without religion; and from the facts of history the laws of human nature can easily be inferred.

Hence education, in order to foster civilization, must foster religion. Now the three great educational agencies are the home, the Church, and the school. These mould men and shape society. Therefore each of them, to do its part well, must foster religion. But many, unfor-

tunately, while avowing that religion should be the light
and the atmosphere of the home and of the Church, are
content to see it excluded from the school, and even
advocate as the best school system that which necessarily
excludes religion.

Few surely will deny that childhood and youth are
the periods of life when the character ought especially
to be subjected to religious influences. Nor can we
ignore the palpable fact that the school is an important
factor in the forming of childhood and youth,—so important that its influence often outweighs that of home
and Church. It cannot, therefore, be desirable or advantageous that religion should be excluded from the
school. On the contrary, it ought there to be one of the
chief agencies for moulding the young life to all that is
true and virtuous, and holy. To shut religion out of the
school, and keep it for home and the Church, is, logically,
to train up a generation that will consider religion good
for home and the Church, but not for the practical business of real life. But a more false and pernicious notion
could not be imagined. Religion, in order to elevate a
people, should inspire their whole life and rule their
relations with one another. A life is not dwarfed, but
ennobled by being lived in the presence of God.

Therefore the school, which principally gives the
knowledge fitting for practical life, ought to be pre-
eminently under the holy influence of religion. From
the shelter of home and school, the youth must soon go
out into the busy ways of trade or traffic or professional
practice. In all these, the principles of religion should
animate and direct him. But he cannot expect to learn
these principles in the work-shop or the office or the
counting-room. Therefore let him be well and thoroughly imbued with them by the joint influences of

home and school, before he is launched out on the dangerous sea of life.

All denominations of Christians are now awaking to this great truth, which the Catholic Church has never ceased to maintain. Reason and experience are forcing them to recognize that the only practical way to secure a Christian people, is to give the youth a Christian education. The avowed enemies of Christianity in some European countries are banishing religion from the schools, in order gradually to eliminate it from among the people. In this they are logical, and we may well profit by the lesson. Hence the cry for Christian education is going up from all religious bodies throughout the land. And this is no narrowness and "sectarianism" on their part; it is an honest and logical endeavor to preserve Christian truth and morality among the people by fostering religion in the young. Nor is it any antagonism to the State; on the contrary, it is an honest endeavor to give to the State better citizens, by making them better Christians. The friends of Christian education do not condemn the State for not imparting religious instruction in the public schools as they are now organized; because they well know it does not lie within the province of the State to teach religion. They simply follow their conscience by sending their children to denominational schools, where religion can have its rightful place and influence.

Two objects therefore, dear brethren, we have in view, to multiply our schools, and to perfect them. We must multiply them, till every Catholic child in the land shall have within its reach the means of education. There is still much to do ere this be attained. There are still thousands of Catholic children in the United States deprived of the benefit of a Catholic school. Pastors and parents should not rest till this defect be remedied. No parish is complete till it has schools adequate to the needs of its children, and the pastor and people of such a parish should feel that they have not accomplished their entire duty until the want is supplied.

But then, we must also perfect our schools. We repudiate the idea that the Catholic school need be in any respect inferior to any other school whatsoever. And if hitherto, in some places, our people have acted on the principle that it is better to have an imperfect Catholic school than to have none, let them now push their praiseworthy ambition still further, and not relax their efforts till their schools be elevated to the highest educational excellence. And we implore parents not to hasten to take their children from school, but to give them all the time and all the advantages that they have the capacity to profit by, so that, in after life, their children may "rise up and call them blessed."

We need hardly remind you, beloved brethren, that while home life would not, as a rule, be sufficient to supply the absence of good or counteract the evil of dangerous influences in the school, it is equally true, that all that the Christian school could accomplish would be inadequate without the co-operation of the Christian home. Christian schools sow the seed, but Christian homes must first prepare the soil, and afterwards foster the seed and bring it to maturity.

. . .

DECREES OF THE COUNCIL—TITLE VI

199. After full consideration of these matters, we conclude and decree:

I.   That near every church a parish school, where one does not yet exist, is to be built and maintained *in perpetuum* within two years of the promulgation of this council, unless the bishop should decide that because of serious difficulties a delay may be granted.

.   .   .

IV.   That all Catholic parents are bound to send their children to the parish school, unless it is evident that a sufficient training in religion is given either in their own homes, or in other Catholic schools; or when because of a sufficient reason, approved by the bishop, with all due precautions and safeguards, it is licit to send them to other schools. What constitutes a Catholic school is left to the decision of the bishop.

5.   Orestes Brownson:
"Catholic Schools and Education"*
(1862)

Wherever whirled the storm of controversy during the mid- and later nineteenth century, invariably within the eye of the storm was Orestes A. Brownson (1803–1876)— editor, essayist, and philosopher. His restless spirit and challenging mind moved uneasily through several religious affiliations until at forty-one he found his home in the Church. The collected writings from his ferocious pen extend to twenty bound volumes, to this day almost unmined ore. He was one of the giants of the Church during the last century. Nearly blind, worn out, but unintimidated by the crescendo of criticism, even from those whose battles he was waging, Brownson closed out his famous review in June 1872 with these words of epitaph: "I am content with the Church as she is. I came to the Church in 1844 in order to be liberated from my bondage to Satan, and to save my soul. It was not so much my intellectual wants as the need of moral helps, of the spiritual assistance of supernatural grace, in recovering moral purity and integrity of life, that led me to her door to beg admission into her communion. I came

* Henry F. Brownson, ed., *The Works of Orestes A. Brownson* (Detroit: Thorndike Nourse, 1884), XII, 496–514; reprinted from *Brownson's Quarterly Review*, Third New York Series, III (January, 1862), 66–84.

not to reform her, but that she might reform me. If I
have even for a moment seemed to forget this, it has
been unconsciously, and I ask pardon of God and man."

The importance of education in general needs in no
sense to be dwelt on in our country, for no people are
or can be more alive to its utility and even necessity than
are the American people, especially in the non-slave-
holding states; and no people have, upon the whole,
made more liberal provisions for its general diffusion.
There would seem to be just as little need of dwelling
on the importance and necessity of Catholic schools and
Catholic education for our Catholic population. All
Catholics feel, or should feel, that education, either under the point of view of religion or of civilization, is
useful and desirable no further than it is Catholic.
Catholic truth is universal truth, is all truth, and no
education not in accordance with it is or can be a true
or a useful education, for error is never useful, but always more or less hurtful. Every Catholic, then, indeed
every man who loves truth and wishes to conform to it,
must be in favor of Catholic schools and Catholic education, if they are Catholic in reality as well as in name.

So believing, our bishops and clergy, supported by
various religious communities, have lost no time in making the imposing effort to provide under their own
direction schools, academies, colleges, and universities
for all our Catholic children and youth. They have felt
the necessity of giving our children a Catholic education,
as the best and surest way of securing their temporal
and spiritual welfare, of promoting Catholic interests,
and of converting this whole country to the Catholic
faith. Yet, strangely enough, they are very far from

receiving the hearty and undivided support of our whole Catholic community. Great dissatisfaction has been expressed, and in quarters entitled to respect, with our colleges and female academies, and not a few whose love of Catholicity and devotion to the church cannot be questioned, refuse to join in the movements for parochial schools, or the establishment of separate schools for our children under the care of our clergy. Whence comes this division of sentiment? Whence comes it that our colleges and conventual schools do not meet the unanimous approbation of Catholic parents and guardians? Whence comes it that so many amongst us prefer the public schools of the country to schools conducted by Catholics? What is the explanation of these facts? How are they to be accounted for? If these schools, whether for the higher or the lower branches of education, are really Catholic, and educate throughout in accordance with Catholic truth, how should it be possible that honest and intelligent Catholics should differ among themselves as to the policy of establishing them, or that any should hesitate to give them their cordial support? These are questions which need and must receive an answer.

There are a great many people, honest people, but not over and above stocked with practical wisdom, who imagine that whatever is done or approved by Catholics in any age or country, in any particular time or locality, must needs be Catholic, and that opposition to it is necessarily opposition to Catholicity itself. These people never doubt that schools and colleges, under the patronage and direction of the bishops, religious orders and congregations, and the regular and secular clergy, must necessarily be truly Catholic in character and tendency, and hence they conclude that dissatisfaction with them or opposition to them must indicate a heterodox ten-

dency, or the absence of a thoroughly Catholic disposition. They transfer to the bishops and clergy as individuals the veneration and respect due only to the
priesthood and the prelacy, and to the individual members of the church the infallibility that can be predicated
only of the church as the living body of Christ. But we
are permitted neither by Catholic faith nor by Catholic
duty to make this transfer, and all experience proves that
there is neither wisdom nor justice in making it. It does
not necessarily follow that schools and colleges are Catholic because founded and directed by religious orders
and congregations approved by the church, or by bishops
and parish priests; and therefore it does not follow that
dissatisfaction with the schools and colleges, or even
opposition to them, is any indication of a heterodox
tendency, or of any want of true Catholic faith and devotion. Such schools may themselves fail to educate in
a truly Catholic spirit, or to give a truly Catholic character to their pupils, and thus leave it possible that the
dissatisfaction or the opposition should arise not from
the fact that they are Catholic, but from the fact that
they are not Catholic, or that, in spite of their name
and profession, they are really sectarian and heterodox.
The dissatisfaction, in such case, instead of being a reproach to those who feel and express it, would be no
mean proof of their Catholic discernment, their strong
desire for really Catholic education, and earnest devotion
to Catholic interests.

There need be no question as to the purity of motive
and honesty of intention on the part of those who are
engaged in founding or supporting schools and colleges
for imparting a Catholic education, or even of those who
tolerate the expression of no opinion adverse to the
system of schools adopted, or to the quality of the

education imparted. The bishops and secular clergy, the religious orders and congregations of both sexes engaged in the work of education, are animated, we doubt not, by the most sincere desire to do good, and are doing what they in their best judgment believe the most likely of anything in their power to promote the interests of our holy religion, and to provide a truly Catholic education for our children. Any hostile criticism which should in any sense impeach their motives or intentions would be manifestly unjust, and should not be tolerated. But the subject of Catholic education itself cannot be prudently withdrawn from discussion, either private or public; nor can its discussion be confined to the prelates and clergy alone. The laity have, to say the least, as deep an interest in it as have ecclesiastics or the religious, and they have in regard to it the common right of all men to judge for themselves. Parents have certain duties growing out of their relation as parents which they cannot throw upon others, and they must themselves discharge them according to the best of their ability. They are bound by the law of God to give their children, as far as in their power, a truly Catholic education, and they are free to criticise and to refuse to support schools, though professing to be Catholic, in which such education is not and cannot be expected to be given. They are not obliged to patronize schools, because founded or directed by Catholics, any more than they are to support a tailoring or a hatting establishment, because owned by a Catholic who employs Catholic workmen, or because recommended by bishops and parish priests. We protest against the assumption that so-called Catholic schools, collegiate or conventual, parochial or private, because under the control of Catholics, participate in the immunities of the church, of the priesthood, or of the prelacy, and are sacred from public investigation and public criticism; or that we are necessarily bound by our Catholic faith and Catholic piety to patronize or defend them any further than we find them Catholic institutions in fact as well as in name.

The first question, then, for us Catholics to settle relates to the catholicity of the education imparted in our so-called Catholic schools. Catholicity, as we have elsewhere shown, is the idea in its plenitude, and therefore the catechism tells us that the church is catholic, because "she subsists in all ages, teaches all nations, and maintains all truth." She, then, is catholic (potentially) in space and time, and (actually) in idea—as she must be, since her life is the life of the Word made flesh, of him who was at once "perfect God and perfect man"— and therefore the whole truth living and individuated in both the divine and human orders in their dialectic union. It is for this reason that the catechism says she "maintains all truth;" and it is because she maintains all truth, and all truth in its unity and integrity, that she is called the *Catholic* Church; and it is because she is catholic in idea, that is, embracing in her ideal all truth, human and divine, that she is actually or potentially catholic in space and time.

Catholic would say *universal,* and when predicated of truth means universal truth, all truth, and all truth in and for all ages and nations. They whose views are not universally true, are not applicable to all times and places, and to all subjects, may have truth under some of its aspects, but they are not Catholics. They are heterodox, sectarian, or national. Men cease to be Catholics, in the full sense of the term, by denying the universality of the idea or life the church is living, the principle she is evolving and actualizing in the life of humanity, and alike whether they deny this universality in relation to space or in relation to time, in relation to the natural, or in relation to the supernatural. They deny Catholicity who deny that it embraces the whole truth in the human order, as they do who deny that it embraces the whole truth in the divine order. To deny it in relation to the natural order is as much to deny Catholicity, as it is to deny it in relation to the supernatural; and we depart as widely from it in denying its catholicity in time, as we do in denying its catholicity in space. The rule of St. Vincent of Lérins says *quod* SEMPER, as well as *quod* UBIQUE.* Catholic truth is simply truth, all truth in the intelligible order and in the super-intelligible, in religion and civilization, in time and eternity, in God and in his creative act.

Catholic education must recognize the catholicity of truth under all its aspects, and tend to actualize it in all the relations of life, in religion and civilization. Its tendency is to aid the church in the fulfilment of her mission, which is the continuous evolution and actualization of the idea, or the life of the Word made flesh, in the life of humanity, or completion in mankind of the incarnation completed in the individual man assumed by the Word. The completion of this work is the complete union of men, through Christ, with God, the finite with the infinite—the true term of human progress, or final cause of the divine creative act. All education, to be Catholic, must tend to this end, the union, without

---

* He refers here to a passage from the fifth-century apologist's *Commonitorium: "In ipsa item catholica ecclesia magnopere curandum est ut id teneamus, quod ubique, quod semper, quod ab omnibus creditum est"* ("Great care must be had that we in the Catholic Church hold the same thing which has been believed everywhere, always, and by all the faithful"). Brownson is stressing the continuity of Catholic belief.—N. G. McC.

absorption of either, or intermixture or confusion of the two natures, of the human and the divine, and therefore of civilization and religion. It must be dialectic, and tend to harmonize all opposites, the creature with the creator, the natural with the supernatural, the individual with the race, social duties with religious duties, order with liberty, authority with freedom, the immutability of the dogma, that is, of the mysteries, with the progress of intelligence, conservatism with reform; for such is the aim of the church herself, and such the mission given her by the Word made flesh, whose spouse she is. Fully and completely up to this idea we expect not education in any age or in any nation to come, but this is the type it should aim to realize, and be constantly and, as far as human frailty admits, actually realizing. Such is the character and tendency of what we term Catholic education.

It is with this ideal standard of Catholic education that we have the right to compare our Catholic schools, and we must judge them as they, by the instruction they give, and the influence they exert, tend or do not tend to its realization. We hazard little in saying that our so-called Catholic schools, in their actual effect, tend rather to depart from this standard than to approach it. They practically fail to recognize human progress, and thus fail to recognize the continuous and successive evolution of the idea in the life of humanity. They practically question the universality of the idea by failing to recognize as Catholic the great principles or ideas natural society is evolving and actualizing in its career through the ages. They do not educate their pupils to be at home and at their ease in their own age and country, or train them to be living, thinking, and energetic men, prepared for the work which actually awaits them in either church or state. As far as we are able to trace the effect of the most approved Catholic education of our days, whether at home or abroad, it tends to repress rather than to quicken the life of the pupil, to unfit rather than to prepare him for the active and zealous discharge either of his religious or his social duties. They who are educated in our schools seem misplaced and mistimed in the world, as if born and educated for a world that has ceased to exist. They come out ignorant of contemporary ideas, contemporary habits of mind, contemporary intelligence and tendencies, and large numbers of them sink into obscurity, and do nothing for their religion or their country; or, what is worse, abandon their religion, turn their backs on the church, and waste all their energies in seeking pleasure, or in accumulating worldly wealth. Of the young men educated in our colleges, a certain number have become priests and religious, and fill the ranks of the clergy and continue the religious orders. Of these we have nothing to say. But, of the others, we would ask: Do we find them up to the level of contemporary civilization, and foremost in all those movements fitted to advance intelligence, morality, and the general well-being of society? Do we find them showing by their superior intelligence, their superior morals, and their loftier aspirations the superiority of their religion and the salutary influence it is fitted to exert on civilization? With very few exceptions, we fear we must answer: This is not the case. Comparatively few of them take their stand as scholars or as men on a level with the graduates of non-Catholic colleges, and those who do take that stand, in most cases, do it by throwing aside nearly all they learned from their alma mater, and adopting the ideas and principles, the modes of thought and action they find in the general civilization of the country in which they live.

Whence comes it that such, in general terms, has been thus far in our country the effect of what we proudly call Catholic education? We cannot ascribe it to any innate incompatibility between Catholic truth and the civilization of the country, for that would be to deny the catholicity of the idea; nor to any repugnance between it and modern society, because that would be to deny its catholicity in time. The cause cannot be in Catholicity itself, nor can it be in our American order of civilization, for Catholicity, if catholic, is adapted to all times and to all nations,—as the catechism tells us, when it says, she "subsists in all ages, and teaches all nations." If we educated in conformity with Catholic truth, those we educate would be fitted for their precise duties in their own time and country, and they would be the active, the living, and the foremost men among their contemporaries and fellow-citizens. When such is not the case, we may be sure that our education fails in some respects, to be Catholic, and is directed to the restoration of a past severed from the present, and therefore an education that breaks the continuity of life either of the church or of humanity; and therefore is essentially a schismatic and heterodox education. It repeats substantially the error of the reformers in the sixteenth century. These reformers may have had honest and even praiseworthy intentions, for there was then in the church, or rather amongst Catholics, as there always is, need enough of reform—deep, thorough, and wide-reaching reform, but they erred fatally in breaking the continuity of the divine-human life, and in aiming either at reproducing an order of things which had passed away, which they called "primitive Christianity," or in leaping to a future which could have no connection with the past, and be no development of what it contained in germ,—the law of all true reform, as of all real progress. The cause of the failure of what we term Catholic education is, in our judgment, in the fact that we educate not for the present or the future, but for a past which can never be restored, and therefore in our education are guilty of a gross anachronism.

We do not mean, and must not be understood to say that the dogmas, that is, the mysteries, as defined in the infallible speech of the church, are not scrupulously taught in all our schools and colleges or that the words of the catechism are not faithfully preserved and duly insisted upon. We concede this, and that this gives to our so-called Catholic schools a merit which no others have or can have. Without the external word, the life of the internal expires, and when it is lost or corrupted, there are no means, except by a new supernatural intervention of Almighty God, of renewing the interior Christian life. This fact is of the first importance, and must never be lost sight of or underrated. The man who has not lost his faith, although his faith is inoperative, or, as theologians say, a "dead faith," is always to be preferred to him who has no faith at all; because he has in him a recuperative principle, and it is more easy to quicken it into activity, than it is to beget faith in one who has it not. The education given in our schools, however defective it may be, must always be preferred to that given in schools in which the dogma is rejected or mutilated, and can never be justly censured, save when compared with its own ideal, or with what it should be and would be, were it truly and thoroughly Catholic.

The fault we find with modern Catholic education is not that it does not faithfully preserve the symbol, that it does not retain all the dogmas or mysteries, so far as

sound words go, but that it treats them as isolated or
dead facts, not as living principles, and overlooks the
fact that the life of the church consists in their continuous evolution and progressive development and
actualization in the life of society and of individuals.
They themselves, since they are principles and pertain
to the ideal the church is evolving and actualizing, must
be immutable, and the same for all times, places, and
men. They are the principles of progress, but not themselves progressive, for the truth was completely expressed
and individuated in the Incarnation. The progress is not
in them, but in their explication and actualization in
the life of humanity. The truth contained in them is
always the same, can neither be enlarged nor diminished;
but our understanding of them may be more or less
adequate, and their explication and application to our
own life and to the life of society may be more or less
complete. Their evolution is successive, progressive, and
continuous. This fact, which lies at the bottom of Dr.
Newman's theory of development, though not always
presented by him in an orthodox sense, is what our
Catholic education seems to us to overlook, and practically to deny. It seems to us to proceed as if the work
of evolution were finished, and there remained nothing
for the Christian to do, but to repeat the past. It aims
not at the continuous evolution and realization of the
Catholic ideal; but to restore a past age, an order of
things which the world has left behind, and which it is
neither possible nor desirable to restore, for it could be
restored, if at all, only as a second childhood. It is now
"behind the times," and unfits rather than prepares the
student for taking an active part in the work of his own
day and generation. It either gives its subjects no work
to do, or a work in which humanity takes no interest

and will not work with them,—a work which all the living and onward tendencies of the age obstinately resist, and which, if there is any truth in what we have said, is adverse alike to the present interests of both religion and civilization.

There can be no question that what generally passes for Catholic education, whether in this or any other country, has its ideal of perfection in the past, and that it resists as un-Catholic, irreligious, and opposed to God, the tendencies of modern civilization. The work that it gives its subjects, or prepares them to perform, is not the work of directing and carrying it forward, or of bringing it into dialectic harmony with religion; but that of re-sisting it, driving it back, anathematizing it as at war with the Gospel, and either of neglecting civilization al-together, and taking refuge in the cloister, in an exclusive or exaggerated asceticism, always bordering on immo-rality, or of restoring a former order of civilization, no longer a living order, and which humanity has evidently left behind, and is resolved shall never be restored.

This, in our judgment, is its great mistake, a mistake that denies the truth of humanity, and virtually con-demns or places in abeyance, the human element of Christianity. It virtually denies the human, because it denies that the human evolves in its life Catholic truth, and pronounces its developments false, its tendencies irreligious, and its irrepressible instincts satanic. We mean that its tendency is in this direction, and hence the manifest and undeniable schism today between the church and humanity, between religion and modern civilization, which, if we understand it, implies a schism between God and man. It runs to one extreme, as ra-tionalistic education runs to another and an opposite ex-treme. Extremes meet. Rationalists condemn the church, because, they say, she is opposed to civilization, and to humanity itself; and many Catholics condemn the civilization humanity in her progress evolves and effects, because, they say, it is opposed to the church, incompatible with religion and the rightful supremacy of God. Both agree as to the fact and the character of the antagonism, and neither seems disposed to inquire whether a medium of reconciliation, of dialectic union, be or be not possible, so that the church, which presupposes humanity, and humanity, which cannot attain to its end, or realize its destiny without the church, may move on in harmony, without any contrariety of will, as there was no contrariety of will between the human and the divine in Christ, the God-man. If there is any truth in Catholicity, or unless our understanding of it be totally false, there is no necessity for this schism either in the nature of the church or in the nature of humanity, and it does and must result only from a defective theology on the one hand, and a false philosophy on the other.

These remarks apply to Catholic education not in our own country only, but throughout no small part of Christendom. In scarcely any part of the Christian world can we find Catholics,—we mean men who are earnest Catholics, firm in their faith, and unfaltering in their devotion to the church,—among the active and influential men of the age. In all, or nearly all countries the Catholic population is the weaker, and the less efficient portion of the population in all that relates to the war of ideas, and the struggle of opinions. Those Catholics who see this and have the courage to place themselves in harmony with the times, are looked upon as, at least, of doubtful orthodoxy, and not unfrequently are held up to clerical denunciation. Even when they are not cried down as heterodox, they are pushed aside as imprudent or unsafe men. It is very widely and, we fear, very generally believed, that true Catholic duty requires us to take our stand for a past civilization, a past order of ideas, and to resist with all our might the undeniable tendencies and instincts of the human race in our day. We are required by the present dominant sentiment of Catholics, to resist progress in every sense and direction, except in the purely ascetic life of individuals, and to content ourselves with the explication and application of the dogmas of the church, the great and immutable principles of Catholic life, given in past times, and embalmed in the opinions of the theologians of other ages, and the dry, technical, and well-nigh unintelligible formulas of the schools. Hence Catholic education, or rather the education adopted and generally approved by Catholics in our age, especially in our country, fails to produce living men, active, thinking men, great men, men of commanding genius, of generous aims, and high and noble aspirations; and hence it also fails to enable the church to take possession of humanity, and to inspire and direct its movements.

But the objection we urge has a peculiar force and application to Catholic education in our country. Our Catholic population, to a great extent, is practically a foreign body and brings with it a civilization foreign from the American, and in some respects inferior to it. The great majority of our congregations are of foreign birth, or the children of foreign-born parents, and the greater part of our bishops and clergy, and of our professors and teachers, have been born, or at least educated, abroad, and they all naturally seek to perpetuate the civilization in which they have been brought up. Those even of our clergy and of our professors and teachers who have been born and educated in the country, have

been educated in schools founded on a foreign model,
and conducted by foreigners, and are, in regard to civilization, more foreign than native. We state the fact as
it is. We are not condemning it; we may regret it, but
we could hardly expect it to be otherwise. The original
settlers of the country were, for the most part, non-
Catholic, and but comparatively few of their descendants
have been or are Catholics. The very large Catholic
population now in the country has not been the growth
of the country, but has been chiefly supplied by a foreign and a very recent migration. This is the fact,—a
fact which is no fault of the Catholic population, but a
fact that must be taken into the account in forming
a judgment of the Catholic education in our own country. Catholics from the Old World necessarily bring with
them their own civilization, which, whether we speak of
France or Italy, Ireland or Germany, is, to say the least,
different from ours, and, in some respects, even hostile
to it.

But this is not all. The civilization they actually bring
with them, and which without intending it they seek
to continue, is, we being judges, of a lower order than
ours. It may be our national prejudice and our ignorance
of other nations, but it is nevertheless our firm conviction, from which we cannot easily be driven, that, regarded in relation to its type, the American civilization
is the most advanced civilization the world has yet seen,
and comes nearer to the realization of the Catholic
ideal than any which has been heretofore developed and
actualized. We speak not of civilization in the sense of
simple *civility*, polish of manners, and personal accomplishments, in which we may not compare always
favorably with the upper classes of other nations; but
of the type or idea we are realizing, our social and politi-

cal constitution, our arrangements to secure freedom and scope for the development and progress of true manhood. In these respects American civilization is, we say not the term of human progress, but, in our judgment, the furthest point in advance as yet reached by any age or nation. Those who come here from abroad necessarily bring with them, therefore, a civilization more or less inferior to it, and which, in relation to it, is a civilization of the past. If they educate, then, according to their own civilization, as they must do, they necessarily educate for a civilization behind the times and below that of the country.

The fact of this inferiority is conceded, or virtually conceded, by our bishops and clergy themselves, in the reason they assign for establishing separate schools for Catholic children. They tell us, and, we must presume, tell us truly, that, if the children of Catholics are educated in the common schools of the country, they will lose their religion and grow up Protestants, or at least non-Catholics. But why so, if the Catholic population represents a civilization not inferior to that represented by the non-Catholic? If Catholic children and Protestant attend the same school, why are the Catholic likely to become Protestant, any more than the Protestant are to become Catholic? The danger alleged could not exist if the Protestant or non-Catholic children did not represent the stronger, and, therefore, the superior civilization. If the Catholic children represented the advancing civilization, the civilization more in accordance with the instincts and tendencies of humanity, and therefore the civilization that has the promise of the future, they would, though inferior in numbers, be the stronger party, and, instead of being themselves perverted, would convert the non-Catholic children, and the opposition to

mixed schools would come from non-Catholic, not from
Catholic parents and guardians. Why is it that so many
of our children, as they grow up and go out into the
world, abandon their religion, lose nearly all memory
of the church of their fathers, live, act, and die as
Protestants or as infidels? You say, and say truly, that it
is owing to the influence of the country; but does not
this show that the civilization of the country is stronger,
more energetic, and more living than that which you
combine, and, to a great extent, insist on combining
with the Catholic dogma?

Will you deny our inference, or seek to escape it by
attributing the fact to the perversity of human nature,
to the seductions of the flesh, and to the temptations
and machinations of the devil? To some extent you may
do so; but you must take care lest you forget or deny the
Catholicity of the Word, and forget or deny that humanity, in the natural order, even though suffering from
the fall, is living the life of the creative Word. The ideal
of humanity which she is realizing in her progress, is
true, an element itself of Catholic truth, and, though
distinguishable, yet inseparable from the ideal the church
is herself realizing in her divine-human life. It will not
do, then, to attribute solely to human perversity, to the
influence of the flesh, or to the machinations of the
devil, the loss of so many of our children as they grow
up; and, therefore, we must maintain that it is in great
measure due to the fact that the civilization which
Catholics bring with them, and with which they associate their Catholic faith, is inferior, and therefore
weaker than the civilization which has been attained to
by humanity in our country, and which, unhappily, instead of being associated with orthodoxy, is associated
with heterodoxy. The civilization of the country does

not owe its superiority to the heterodoxy with which it is associated, any more than the civilization which Catholics bring with them owes its inferiority to the orthodoxy with which it is accidentally associated. The civilization of the country owes its superiority to the truth which it accepts and evolves, and is weakened and prevented from attaining to its full development by its association with heterodoxy, as orthodoxy itself is weakened and prevented from gaining the successes it is entitled to, by being associated with an inferior civilization.

The inferiority of the civilization associated in our country with orthodoxy might be inferred *a priori* from the fact that the mass of our Catholic population are from the more uncultivated classes of the Old World, with whom it would be ridiculous to pretend that civilization has reached its highest point of development. Whatever respect we may have for the peasantry of Ireland or Germany, how much soever we may honor them for the firmness with which, under the severest trials and temptations, they have held fast to the orthodox faith, we can by no means take them in respect of civilization as the advance-guard of humanity. But the facts themselves, facts which nobody can question, sufficiently prove, at least as to our English-speaking Catholics, that their civilization is of an inferior order. Their sympathies are far closer with the slaveholding South than with the free North, and we need not add that the civilization of the free North is far superior to that represented by the slaveholding South. The civilization of the South is based on slavery as its corner-stone, and slavery is the very essence of barbarism. The distinction between barbarism and civilization is precisely the distinction between slavery and liberty. The true American civilization has its type and seat in the free states, and is best represented by the Puritans and their descendants, who were in fact its chief founders as they are its chief, or, at least, most earnest supporters. Yet, except with a certain number of converts of New England birth and descent, we rarely find a Catholic who does not look upon Puritan New England as the most anti-Catholic portion of the Union, and consider that his best way of promoting Catholic interests is to fight against her.

The great body of our Catholics, no doubt, wish to americanize, and conform to the civilization of the country, but they have hitherto americanized, so far as they have americanized at all, in a southern rather than in a northern sense. The type of the Americanism they aim to adopt is in Maryland, not in Massachusetts; Baltimore, not Boston; and nothing can exceed the hostility of the Maryland type, which, properly speaking, is the Virginia type, to the Boston, or New England type. Indeed, it is these two orders of civilization that meet in mortal combat in the civil war which now threatens the integrity of the American nation. The war is a struggle for life and death, a struggle between a civilization based on slavery, represented by the South, and a civilization based on constitutional liberty and the rights of men, represented by the free states. And, in this struggle, if, as is the fact, the interest and loyalty of Catholics lead them in large numbers to take sides with the North, their sympathies are very generally with the South; and we cannot doubt that, if the South were the loyal party, they would much more readily fight with the South than they now fight with the North. Even, then, where our Catholics aim to be American, it is not American in the sense of the highest, truest, and most advanced Americanism; but in the sense of the lowest, the least advanced, that which is least remote from barbarism, and the furthest removed from that which the church as well as humanity demands, and never ceases to struggle to obtain.

We are also borne out in our views by the political history of the country. Politically, the southern leaders have for a long time formed their association with the least intelligent, the least advanced classes in the free states, and these southern leaders are those our Catholic population have followed with the most alacrity. This fact proves, on the one hand, that the South represents the lowest order of civilization in the country, and that Catholics are more easily engaged in supporting it than in supporting the superior civilization represented by the northern states. It is not too much to say that the great influx of the Catholic peasantry of different European states into the country, and the conferring on them, almost on their arrival, of political franchises, have done not a little to corrupt our politics, and to lower the standard of our civilization. Their orthodoxy, as yet, has done less to advance, than their inferior civilization has done to corrupt and lower, our civilization and morals. However humiliating this fact may be to us as Catholics, there is no use in attempting to deny it, or to disguise it. It is a fact which all intelligent Americans see and know, and it is one which we ourselves should dare look in the face. The opposition to us represented by "Native-American," or "Know-Nothing" parties or movements, is not opposition to us as orthodox Catholics, nor, in itself considered, to us as foreigners, but simply as representatives of a civilization different from the American, and, in many respects, inferior and opposed to it. We have practically, if not theoretically, insisted that our orthodoxy and our foreign and inferior civilization are inseparable; and the heterodox American people have in this agreed with us, and hence their opposition to us, and ours to them. Heterodoxy, with the heterodox of our country, is no longer a living principle, and is retained only because associated, accidentally associated, with a superior and more advanced civilization. Orthodoxy is opposed not because there is any opposition to it on its own account, but because it is believed to be inseparably wedded to that inferior and less advanced civilization that has come hither with it from the Old World, and which many honest Catholics think, if they ever think at all on the subject, is identical with it.

Now, the objection to Catholic schools, especially those for the people at large, is that they tend, and for a time at least must tend, to perpetuate the association of orthodoxy with this inferior civilization, and thus injure alike the country and the church. These schools must be taught chiefly by foreigners, or, if not by foreigners, at least by those whose sympathies and connections, tastes and habits are un-American; because what is wanted by their founders and supporters is not simply the preservation of orthodoxy, but the perpetuation of the foreignism hitherto associated with it. Schools which should associate real Americanism with orthodoxy would be hardly less offensive or more acceptable to them than the public schools themselves. They must, therefore, be conducted and taught by men who will keep up the old association, and prevent the association of real Americanism with orthodoxy. Yet it is precisely this latter association which is desirable both for civilization and for religion, and it is only by breaking the old associations, and forming the new in good faith, as we are in fact required to do by orthodoxy itself, that Catholics can cease to be in this country an isolated foreign colony, or a band of emigrants encamped for the night, and ready to strike their tents, and take up their line of march on the morrow for some other place.

These are some of the reasons which have led many of our most intelligent, most earnest, and devout Catholics to form their unfavorable judgment of Catholic schools and Catholic education, as they now are, and for some time are likely to be, in the United States. They are solid reasons as far as they go, and fully justify the dissatisfaction with them we began by recognizing. They prove that here and elsewhere, but especially here, Catholic education, or the education given by Catholics, is below the wants of the age and country, and prove that, from the seminary down to the primary school, it stands in need, whether we consult the interest of orthodoxy or that of civilization, of a wide, deep, and thorough reform. Yet, after long reflection and much hesitation, some would say opposition, we must say that we do not regard them as sufficient reasons for abandoning the movement for Catholic schools and education supported by our bishops and clergy. It may be that the movement was premature, and that it would have been better to have used for a longer time the schools of the country, as the early Christians did those of the empire, before attempting to establish schools of our own, save for the education of the clergy. But it is too late to discuss that question now. The movement has, wisely or unwisely, been set on foot, and gone too far to be arrested, even if it were desirable to arrest it. Our bishops and clergy have decided that the movement shall go on, and the Catholic cause can never be promoted by any anti-hierarchical action. Much good may be done that is not done by or under the direction of the hierarchy; but no good end can ever be obtained in opposition to it. This consideration is of itself sufficient to deter us from opposing the movement, and of inducing us to accept it at least as *un fait accompli,* and to make the best we can of it.

That we are to have schools and colleges of our own, under the control of Catholics, we take it is a "fixed fact." Whether the movement for them is premature or not, it is idle, if nothing worse, to war against it. Let us say, then, to those who regard the education actually given by Catholics as we do, and who have not seen their way clear to the support of primary schools under the control of Catholics as a substitute, in the case of Catholic children, for the common schools of the country, that we regard it as our duty now to accept the movement, and labor not to arrest it, or to embarrass it, but to reform and render truly Catholic the whole system of Catholic education, from the highest grade to the lowest. Let it be our work not to destroy Catholic education, but to reform and advance it. The first care of all Catholics should be the preservation of orthodoxy, and, in the actual state of our Catholic population, it may be that orthodoxy will be better preserved by schools under Catholic direction than it can be by sending our children to the public schools. The objections we have set forth are, after all, only temporary and accidental. They grow out of the present and past state of our Catholic population, and must disappear under the slow but effectual operation of time and causes already in operation amongst us. We might gain something under the point of view of civilization by adopting the schools of the country; but, as our prelates and clergy are strongly opposed to them, and have done much to bring them into disrepute with Catholics, we should probably lose, under the point of view of orthodoxy, more than would thus be gained. Schools under the control of Catholics will, at least, teach the catechism, and though they may in fact teach it as a dead letter, rather than as a quickening spirit, it is better that it should be taught as a dead letter than not be taught at all. It is only by preserving the dogma intact that we do or can preserve the Christian ideal, or have the slightest chance of securing our final destiny. The hopes of the world for time and eternity are dependent on the preservation of the orthodox faith.

The reform in our schools and in education will go on just in proportion as it goes on in our Catholic community itself, and perhaps even much faster. The dissatisfaction we hear expressed with our collegiate education for boys, and with that of our conventual schools for girls, is an encouraging symptom; it proves that there is, after all, a growing americanization of our Catholic population, and that the need of an education less European and more truly American is daily becoming more widely and more deeply felt. It will be more widely and more deeply felt still as time goes on, and as Catholics become more generally naturalized in habit, feeling, and association, as well as in law. It indicates also the revival of Catholic life in our population, that Catholics are becoming more earnest and living men, and unwilling that their orthodoxy should be wrapped up in a clean napkin and buried in the earth. In proportion as their Catholic life revives and grows more active, they will demand an education more in accordance with Catholic truth in all its branches, than is that now given. The demand will create a supply. And when the present civil strife is over, the integrity of the nation reëstablished, and American civilization has proved itself capable of subduing the barbarism of the South, and of marching onward and upward with humanity, in her career of progress to union with the infinite, we trust Catholics will find and

feel themselves real Americans, differing from other
Americans only in the respect that orthodoxy differs from
heterodoxy, truth from error, life from death. Then our
schools will assume their true character and position, and
exert a truly Catholic influence. They will preserve
orthodoxy not as a dead letter, not as isolated and inoperative dogma, but as a quickening spirit, as living
and operative truth. Then, under the point of view of
civilization, instead of tending to recall a dead past, they
will accept the living present, and associate the living
civilization of the day with the orthodox faith,—reunite
in a living and productive whole the scattered members
of the torn and bleeding body of truth, and aid both the
church and the nation in carrying forward our civilization
to the last term of its progress. Then our schools will
send out living men, live with the love of God and of
man,—men of large minds, of liberal studies, and generous aims,—men inspired by faith and genius, who will
take the command of their age, breathe their whole souls
into it, inform it with their own love of truth, and raise
it to the level of their own high and noble aspirations.
Let us console ourselves for what Catholic education
now is with what it may become, and with what we may
by well-directed effort aid it in becoming. This is the
conclusion to which we ourselves have come, and if we
are not satisfied with Catholic schools and education as
they are, we are satisfied with their capabilities, and shall
henceforth content ourselves with doing what in us lies
to bring them under the great law of progress, which we
have insisted on, and which is the law of all life, even of
the divine life,—as is proved in the eternal generation of
the Word, and the procession of the Holy Ghost, or in the
assertion of theologians that "God is most pure act,"
actus purissimus.

6. Instruction of the Congregation of Propaganda de Fide* (1875)

The passing of years had only made the school situation graver. The Second Plenary Council of Baltimore had simply exhorted the bishops "to see that schools be established in connection with all the churches of their dioceses. . . ."† To impress upon the faithful the seriousness of the matter and to strengthen their own authority in persuading pastors to build parish schools, a number of the bishops requested a formal document from the Roman Congregation for the Propagation of the Faith. The Instruction printed here explains in part the vigor of the decrees on establishing schools passed by the Third Plenary Council (see pp. 93–94).

The Sacred Congregation of Propaganda has been many times assured that for the Catholic children of the United

* "Instruction of the Congregation of Propaganda de Fide Concerning Catholic Children Attending American Public Schools, November 24, 1875," in John Tracy Ellis, ed., *Documents of American Catholic History* (Milwaukee, Wis.: The Bruce Publishing Co., 1956), pp. 417–420. The Latin text appeared in *Acta et decreta concilii plenarii Baltimorensis tertii* (Baltimore: John Murphy & Co., 1886), pp. 279–282; the English translation here reprinted was first published in *The Pastor*, IV (June, 1886), 232–237.

† *Concilium plenarium totius Americae septentrionalis foederatae Baltimori habitum anno 1852* (Baltimore: John Murphy & Co., 1853), p. 47.

States of America evils of the gravest kind are likely to result from the so-called public schools.

The sad intelligence moved the Propaganda to propose to the illustrious prelates of that country a series of questions, with the object of ascertaining, first, why the faithful permit their children to attend non-catholic schools, and secondly, what may be the best means of keeping the young away from schools of this description. The answers, as drawn up by the several prelates, were submitted, owing to the nature of the subject, to the Supreme Congregation of the Holy Office. The decision reached by their Eminences, Wednesday, June 30, 1875, they saw fit to embody in the following *Instruction,* which the Holy Father graciously confirmed on Wednesday, November 24, of the same year.

1.   The first point to come under consideration was the system of education itself, quite peculiar to those schools. Now, that system seemed to the S. Congregation most dangerous and very much opposed to Catholicity. For the children in those schools, the very principles of which exclude all religious instruction, can neither learn the rudiments of the faith nor be taught the precepts of the Church; hence, they will lack that knowledge, of all else, necessary to man without which there is no leading a Christian life. For children are sent to these schools from their earliest years, almost from their cradle; at which age, it is admitted, the seeds sown of virtue or of vice take fast root. To allow this tender age to pass without religion is surely a great evil.

2.   Again, these schools being under no control of the Church, the teachers are selected from every sect indiscriminately; and this, while no proper precaution is taken to prevent them injuring the children, so that there is nothing to stop them from infusing into the young

minds the seeds of error and vice. Then evil results are certainly to be dreaded from the fact that in these schools, or at least in very many of them, children of both sexes must be in the same class and class-room and must sit side by side at the same desk. Every circumstance mentioned goes to show that the children are fearfully exposed to the danger of losing their faith and that their morals are not properly safeguarded.

3. Unless this danger of perversion can be rendered remote, instead of proximate, such schools cannot in conscience be used. This is the dictate of natural as well as of divine law. It was enunciated in unmistakable terms by the Sovereign Pontiff, in a letter addressed to a former Archbishop of Freiburg, July 14, 1864. He thus writes: "There can be no hesitation; wherever the purpose is afoot or carried out of shutting out the Church from all authority over the schools, there the children will be sadly exposed to loss of their faith. Consequently the Church should, in such circumstances, not only put forth every effort and spare no pains to get for the children the necessary Christian training and education, but would be further compelled to remind the faithful and publicly declare that schools hostile to Catholicity cannot in conscience be attended." These words only express a general principle of natural and divine law and are consequently of universal application wherever that most dangerous system of training youth has been unhappily introduced.

4. It only remains, then, for the prelates to use every means in their power to keep the flocks committed to their care from all contact with the public schools. All are agreed that there is nothing so needful to this end as the establishment of Catholic schools in every place,—and schools no whit inferior to the public ones. Every effort, then, must be directed towards starting Catholic schools

where they are not, and, where they are, towards enlarg-
ing them and providing them with better accommoda-
tions and equipment until they have nothing to suffer, as
regards teachers or equipment, by comparison with the
public schools. And to carry out so holy and necessary a
work, the aid of religious brotherhoods and of sisterhoods will be found advantageous where the bishop sees
fit to introduce them. In order that the faithful may the
more freely contribute the necessary expenses, the bishops
themselves should not fail to impress on them, at every
suitable occasion, whether by pastoral letter, sermon or
private conversation, that as bishops they would be recre-
ant to their duty if they failed to do their very utmost to
provide Catholic schools. This point should be especially
brought to the attention of the more wealthy and influential Catholics and members of the legislature.

5.   In that country there is no law to prevent Catholics
having their own schools and instructing and educating
their youth in every branch of knowledge. It is therefore
in the power of Catholics themselves to avert, with God's
help, the dangers with which Catholicity is threatened
from the public school system. Not to have religion and
piety banished from the school-room is a matter of the
very highest interest, not only to certain individuals and
families, but to the entire country,—a country now so
prosperous and of which the Church has had reason to
conceive such high hopes.

6.   However, the S. Congregation is not unaware that
circumstances may be sometimes such as to permit parents conscientiously to send their children to the public
schools. Of course they cannot do so without having sufficient cause. Whether there be sufficient cause in any particular case is to be left to the conscience and judgment of
the bishop. Generally speaking, such cause will exist

when there is no Catholic school in the place, or the one
that is there cannot be considered suitable to the condition and circumstances in life of the pupils. But even in
these cases, before the children can conscientiously attend
the public school, the danger, greater or less, of perversion, which is inseparable from the system, must be
rendered remote by proper precaution and safeguards.
The first thing to see to, then, is whether the danger of
perversion, as regards the school in question, is such as
cannot possibly be rendered remote; as, for instance,
whether the teaching there is such, or the doings of a
nature so repugnant to Catholic belief and morals, that
ear cannot be given to the one, nor part taken in the
other without grievous sin. It is self-evident that danger
of this character must be shunned at whatever cost, even
life itself.

7. Further, before a child can be conscientiously
placed at a public school, provision must be made for
giving it the necessary Christian training and instruction,
at least out of school hours. Hence parish priests and missionaries in the United States should take seriously to
heart the earnest admonitions of the Council of Baltimore, and spare no labor to give children thorough
catechetical instructions, dwelling particularly on those
truths of faith and morals which are called most in question by Protestants and unbelievers: children beset with
so many dangers they should guard with tireless vigilance,
induce them to frequent the sacraments, excite in them
devotion to the Blessed Virgin and on all occasions animate them to hold firmly by their religion. The parents or
guardians must look carefully after those children. They
must examine them in their lessons, or if not able themselves, get others to do it. They must see what books they
use and, if the books contain passages likely to injure the

child's mind, explain the matter. They must keep them
from freedom and familiarity with those of the other
school children whose company might be dangerous to
their faith or morals, and absolutely away from the corrupt.

8.   Parents who neglect to give this necessary Christian training and instruction to their children, or who
permit them to go to schools in which the ruin of their
souls is inevitable, or finally, who send them to the public
school without sufficient cause and without taking the
necessary precautions to render the danger of perversion
remote, and do so while there is a good and well-equipped
Catholic school in the place, or the parents have the
means to send them elsewhere to be educated,—that such
parents, if obstinate, cannot be absolved, is evident from
the moral teaching of the Church.

7. John Ireland:
"State Schools and Parish Schools"*
(1890)

At the 1889 convention of the National Educational Association in Nashville, Cardinal James Gibbons of Baltimore and Bishop John J. Keane, first rector of the newly opened Catholic University of America, gave papers entitled "Should Americans Educate Their Children in Denominational Schools?" Two additional papers were contributed to the discussion on denominational schools: "Has the Parochial School Proper Place in America?" by Edwin Mead of Boston and "Public and Parochial Schools" by John Jay of New York.† The outcome of the conference was judged by the two Catholic speakers to have been generally beneficial: a large and influential body of educators had heard a sound presentation of the Catholic position, and some valid questions had been raised relative to fitting the parochial school into the American context. The next year Archbishop Ireland of St. Paul was invited to address the same national meeting when it convened in his see city.‡ His compromise ap-

* John Ireland, *The Church and Modern Society* (Chicago: D. H. McBride & Co., 1896), I, 197–214.

† The four papers were published in a pamphlet entitled *Denominational Schools* (Syracuse, N.Y.: C. W. Bardeen, 1889).

‡ John Ireland (1838–1918), an immigrant boy who became a true giant of the American Church and State, was also a world figure. With his energy and keen sense of social and political realities, he

*proach, which would have provided religious instruction
and made parish schools a part of the public system, un-
loosed a controversy among Catholic leaders that "was
without parallel in American Catholic history, in point
of extent, intensity, and bitterness of feeling."**

I beg leave to make at once my profession of faith.
I declare unbounded loyalty to the constitution of my
country. I desire no favors; I claim no rights that are not
in consonance with its letter and spirit. The rights which
the constitution guarantees I do claim, and, in doing
so, I am but the truer and more loyal American. In what
I am about to say to this distinguished audience the principles of our common American citizenship will inspire
my words. I beg you to listen to me, and to discuss my
arguments in the light of those principles.

I am a friend and an advocate of the state school.
In the circumstances of the present time I uphold the
parish school. I sincerely wish that the need for it did
not exist. I would have all schools for the children of the
people to be state schools.

The accusation has gone abroad that Catholics are
bent on destroying the state school. Never was accusation
more unfounded. I will summarize the articles of my

---

became a symbol of the young American republic. On social questions, his heart beat in close concert with that of the aged Leo
XIII. Of the pontiff's fondness for Ireland, the pope's legate Archbishop Satolli could say in St. Paul: "That while holding in veneration and love all the prelates of the American Church, yet he [Leo] has
a special esteem and affection for your Archbishop, whose personal
fame has made the city's name like unto itself. . . ." Quoted in Daniel
F. Reilly, *The School Controversy (1891–1893)* (Washington, D.C.:
The Catholic University of America Press, 1943), p. 205.

   * Allen Sinclair Will, *Life of James Cardinal Gibbons, Archbishop
of Baltimore* (New York: E. P. Dutton & Co., 1922), II, 238.

school creed; they follow all the lines upon which the state school is built.

The right of the state school to exist is, I consider, a matter beyond the stage of discussion. I fully concede it. I go farther: I concede the necessity of the state school. The child must have instruction, and in no mean degree, if the man is to earn for himself an honest competence, and acquit himself of the duties which, for its own life and prosperity, society exacts from all its members. This proposition, which is true in any country of modern times, is peculiarly true in America. The imparting of such instruction is primarily the function of the parent.

The divine appointment is that under the care and direction of the parent the child shall grow in mind as well as in body. But, as things are, tens of thousands of children will not be instructed if parents solely remain in charge of the duty. The State must come forward as an agent of instruction; else ignorance will prevail. Indeed, in the absence of state action there never was that universal instruction which we have so nearly attained, and which we deem so necessary. In the absence of state action universal instruction would, I believe, never have been possible in any country.

Universal instruction implies free schools in which knowledge is to be had for the asking; in no other manner can instruction be brought within the reach of all children. Free schools! Blest indeed is the nation whose vales and hillsides they adorn, and blest the generations upon whose souls are poured their treasures! No tax is more legitimate than that which is levied in order to dispel mental darkness, and build up within the nation's bosom intelligent manhood and womanhood. The question should not be raised: How much good accrues to

the individual tax payer? It suffices that the general welfare is promoted. It is scarcely necessary to add that the
money paid in school tax is the money of the State, and
is to be disbursed only by the officials of the State, and
only for the specific purposes for which it was collected.

I am unreservedly in favor of state laws making instruction compulsory. Instruction is so much needed by the
citizen for his own sake and for that of society that the
parent who neglects to provide for the education of the
child sins against the child and against society, and should
be punished by the State. First principles, of course, must
not be forgotten. Since instruction is primarily the function of the parent, the parent possesses the right to educate his child in the manner agreeable to himself, provided always that the education given in this manner
suffices to fit the child for his ulterior duties to society.
Only when children do not attend other schools known
to be competent to impart instruction, should compulsory
education demand attendance in state schools. The compulsory laws recently enacted in certain states of the
Union are, in my judgment, objectionable in a few of
their incidental clauses. These clauses will, I am confident, be readily altered in future legislative sessions. With
the body of the laws, and their general intent to ensure
universal instruction, I am in most hearty accord.

It were idle for me to praise the work of the state
school of America in imparting secular instruction. We
all recognize its value. It is our pride and our glory. The
Republic of the United States has solemnly affirmed its
resolve that within its borders no clouds of ignorance shall
settle upon the minds of the children of its people. In
furnishing the means to accomplish this result its generosity knows no limit. The free school of America!
Withered be the hand raised in sign of its destruction!

Can I be suspected of enmity to the state school because I would fain widen the expanse of its wings until all the children of the people find shelter beneath their cover; because I tell of defects which for very love of the state school I seek to remedy?

I turn to the denominational or parish school. It exists. I again express my regret that there is a necessity for its existence. In behalf of the state school I call upon my fellow-Americans to aid in the removal of this necessity.

Catholics are foremost in establishing parish schools— seven hundred and fifty thousand children, it is estimated, are educated in their parish schools. Only a lack of material means prevents them from housing the full number of their children. Lutherans, also, exhibit great zeal for parish schools. Many Episcopalians, and not a few of other Protestant denominations, commend and organize parish schools. The various denominational colleges of the country are practically parish schools for the children of the richer classes. The spirit of the parish school, if not the school itself, is widespread among American Protestants, and is made manifest by their determined opposition to the exclusion of Scripture-reading and other devotional exercises from the school-room.

There is dissatisfaction with the state school as it is at present organized. The state school tends to eliminate religion from the minds and hearts of the youth of the country.

This is my grievance against the state school of to-day. Believe me, my Protestant fellow-citizens, I am absolutely sincere, when I declare that I speak for the weal of Protestantism as well as for that of Catholicism. I am a Catholic, of course, to the tiniest fibre of my heart, unflinching and uncompromising in my faith. But God forbid that I should desire to see in America the ground which Protestantism now occupies swept by the devastating blast of unbelief. Let me be your ally in warding off from the country irreligion, the destroyer of Christian life and of Christian civilization. What we have to fear is the materialism that does not see beyond the universe a living personal God, and the agnosticism that reduces Him to an unknown perhaps. Irreligion is abroad, scorning the salvation which is offered in the teachings and graces of Christ Jesus, sneering at the Biblical page, warring upon the sacredness of the Christian Sabbath and the music of its church bells that tell of Heaven and of the hopes of immortal souls. Let us be on our guard. In our fear lest Protestants gain some advantage over Catholics, or Catholics over Protestants, we play into the hands of unbelievers and secularists. We have given over to them the school, the nursery of thought. Are we not securing to them the mastery of the future?

The state school is non-religious. There never can be positive religious teaching where the principle of non-sectarianism rules. What is the result? The school deals with immature, childish minds, upon which silent facts and examples make deepest impression. It claims nearly all the time remaining to pupils outside of rest and recreation. It treats of land and sea, but not of Heaven; it speaks of statesmen and warriors, but not of God and Christ; it tells how to attain success in this world, but says nothing about the world beyond the grave. The pupil sees and listens, and insensibly forms the conclusion that religion is of minor importance. Religious indifference becomes his creed; his manhood will be, as was his childhood in the school, estranged from God and the positive influences of religion. The brief and hurried lessons of the family fireside and the Sunday school will be of slight avail. At best, the time is too short for that most difficult of lessons, religion. The child is weary after the exacting drill of the schoolroom, and does not relish an extra task, of the necessity of which the teacher, in whom he confides most trustingly, has said nothing. The great mass of children receive no fireside lessons, and attend no Sunday school, and the great mass of the children of America are growing up without religion. Away with theories and dreams: let us read the facts.

In ten thousand homes of the land the father hastens to his work at early dawn, before his children have risen from their slumbers, and at night an exhausted frame bids him seek repose, with scarcely time to kiss his little ones. The mother toils all day, that her children may eat and be clothed; it is mockery to ask her to be their teacher! What may we expect from the Sunday school? An hour in the week to study religion is as nothing, and during that hour the small number only will be present. The churches are open and the teachers are at hand, but the non-religious school has engrossed the attention and the energies of the child during five days of the week; he is unwilling to submit to the drudgery of a further hour's work on Sunday. Accidentally, it may be, and unintentionally, but, in fact, most certainly, the state school crowds out the Church. The teaching of religion is not a function of the state; but the State should, for the sake of its people, and for its own sake, permit and facilitate the teaching of religion by the Church. This the State does not do; rather, it hinders and prevents the work of the Church. The children of the masses are learning no religion. The religion of thousands who profess some form of religion, is the merest veneering of mind and heart. Its doctrines are vague and chaotic notions as to what God is, and what our relations to Him are. Very often it is mere sentimentality, and its precepts are the decorous rulings of natural culture and natural prudence. This is not the religion that built up our Christian civilization in the past and that will maintain it in the future. This is not the religion that will subjugate passion and repress vice. It is not the religion that will guard the family and save society.

Let the State look to itself. The mind which it polishes is a two-edged sword—an instrument for evil as well as for good; it were fatal to polish it without the assurance that in all likelihood it shall become an instrument for good. I am not questioning how far we may lay at the door of the non-religious school the breaking up of Christian creeds, the growth of agnosticism and unbelief, the weakening of public and private morals, and the almost complete estrangement from church organizations of the poor and the working classes. But I do submit that these dreaded evils of our day should awaken us from our lethargy, and stimulate us to bestow more than ordinary care upon the religious instruction of the children of the land, that they may have the strength to withstand the fierce temptations which await them.

Do not say that the state school teaches morals. Christians demand religion. From the principles of religion, morals derive power and vitality. Separated from a belief in God, and in the existence of the soul beyond the present life, morals are vague and weak commands which passion is not slow to scorn. What seem to be morals without religion are often but the blossomings of fortunate and kindly natures, or habits, which, fashioned upon Christian traditions, grow weak as the traditions become remote.

To the American people—religious-minded and God-fearing as I know them to be—I put the question: Ought we not to have religious instruction in connection with the school? There are, I confess, serious difficulties in the way. But are we to be stopped by difficulties, when it is incumbent upon us to reach the goal?

Secularists and unbelievers will demand their rights. I concede their rights. I will not impose upon them my religion, which is Christianity. But let them not impose upon me and my fellow-Christians their religion, which is secularism. Secularism is a religion of its kind, and usually a very loud-spoken and intolerant religion. Non-sectarianism is not secularism, and, when non-sectarianism is intended, the secularist sect must not claim for itself the field which it refuses to others. I am taking my stand upon our common American citizenship. The liberty I claim, that I grant.

I come to the chief difficulty. The American people at large are Christians; but they are divided among themselves. Not to speak of other differences, there is the vital and radical one between Catholicism and Protestantism of all forms. I am not arguing; I am stating facts. Well-meaning men propose as a remedy to teach a common Christianity in the schools. This will not do. In loyalty to their principles, Catholics cannot and will not accept a common Christianity. To Catholics, what does not bear on its face the stamp of Catholicity is Protestant in form and in implication, even if it be Catholic in substance. This being a settled fact, American Catholics will not, of course, impose Catholicism upon Protestant children, and, with similar fair-mindedness, American Protestants will not impose Protestantism upon Catholic children. A compromise becomes necessary. Is it not a thousand times better to make a compromise than to allow secularism to triumph and own the country?

I turn to all Americans—secularists as well as Christian

believers—I address them in the name of American citizenship. We are a practical people, and when we find facts before us, whether we like or dislike them, we look at them with an eye to the general good. Now, it is manifest that dissatisfaction exists with the state school, because of its exclusion of religion. This dissatisfaction, moreover, is founded on conscience, and will continue until the cause of it is removed.

Is not the fact that dissatisfaction exists sufficient for Americans to set to work earnestly, and with a good will, to remove the cause of it? The welfare of the country demands peace and harmony among citizens. Let us put an end to the constant murmurings and bitter recriminations with which our school war fills the land. Since we prize the advantages of our state school, let us enable all the children of the people to enjoy those advantages. Since there is such a public institution as the state school, supported by all the people, let us see that all may use it—let there be no taxation without representation in the enjoyment of the benefits of it.

I invoke the spirit of American liberty and American institutions. Citizens of the Republic may differ diametrically in their views of policies and measures; some may deem the views of others to be utterly wrong. Still, is it not the duty of all to promote peace, and, as far as possible, to make concessions so that none be dissatisfied or disturbed in their rights of conscience? It matters not that one of the parties to a controversy comprises the majority of the voters of the State. The force of numbers may prevail in civil law: it is not always justice. Minorities have rights, and those rights the majority should recognize as speedily as may be consistent with the public weal. It is no honor to America that ten millions of its people are forced by law to pay taxes for the support of schools to which their conscience does not give approval, and are, furthermore, compelled, by their zeal for the religious instruction of their children, to build schoolhouses of their own, and pay their own teachers. It is no honor for the fifty millions to profit by the taxes paid by the ten millions. The cry that the state schools are open to Catholics, if they silence their conscience, is not a defense that will hold before the bar of justice. This aspect of the case is the more serious when we consider that the ten millions are largely the poorer classes of the population, and that they are sincerely and loyally desiring to obtain the benefits of the state school, if only the obstacles be removed.

It is no honor to the American Republic that she, more than any other nation, be eager to keep religion away from schools. No nation goes in this direction so far as ours. It is a terrible experiment upon which we have entered; the very life of our civilization and of our country is at stake. I know not how to account for this condition of things. Neither the genius nor the history of the country gives countenance to it. The American people are naturally reverent and religious. Their laws and public observances breathe forth the perfume of religion. The American school, as it first reared its log walls amid the villages of New England, was religious through and through. The favor with which a non-religious school is now regarded is, I verily believe, due to the thoughtlessness of a moment, and will not last.

I solve the difficulty by submitting it to the calm judgment of the country. No question is insoluble to Americans, if truth and justice press it home to them. Other countries, whose civilization we do not despise, have found a solution. I instance England and Prussia. We are not inferior to those countries in practical legislation and in the spirit of peaceful compromise. Suggestions of mine must necessarily be crude in form, and local and temporary in application. I will, however, lay them before you. I would permeate the regular state school with the religion of the majority of the children of the land, be this religion as Protestant as Protestantism can be, and I would, as is done in England, pay for the secular instruction given in denominational schools according to results; that is, every pupil passing the examination before state officials, and in full accordance with the state program, would secure to his school the cost of the tuition of a pupil in the state school. This is not paying for religious instruction, but for the secular instruction demanded by the state, and given to the pupil as thoroughly as he could have received it in the state school.

Another plan: I would do as Protestants and Catholics in Poughkeepsie and other places in the United States have agreed to do, to the entire satisfaction of all citizens and the great advancement of educational interests. In Poughkeepsie the city school board rents the buildings formerly used as parish schools, and from the hour of 9 A.M. to that of 3 P.M. the school is in every respect a state school—teachers being engaged and paid by the board, teachers and pupils being examined, state books being used, the door being always open to superintendent and members of the board. There is simply the tacit understanding that so long as the teachers, Catholic in faith, pass their examinations and do their work as efficiently and as loyally as other teachers under the control of the board, they shall not be replaced by teachers of another faith. During school hours no religious instruction is given. Christian doctrine is taught outside the hours for which the buildings are leased to the board. The State pays not one cent for the religious instruction of the pupils. In the other schools, Protestant devotional exercises take place in fullest freedom before the usual school hour.*

Do not tell me of difficulties of detail in the working out of either of my schemes. There are difficulties; but will not the result be ample compensation for the struggle to overcome them? Other schemes, more perfect in conception and more easy of application, will, perhaps, be presented later; meanwhile, let trial be made of those which I have submitted.

Allow me one word as a Catholic. I have sought to place on the precise line where it belongs the objection which Catholics have to the state school. Is it fair, is it honest, to raise the cry that Catholics are opposed to education, to free schools, to the American school system? I lose patience with adversaries who seek to place us in this false position, so opposed to all our convictions and resolves. In presence of this vast and distinguished assembly, I protest with all the energy of my soul against the charge that the schools of the Nation have their enemies among Catholics. Not one stone of the wondrous

---

* The plan which is here sketched is the so-called Irish plan. It has been in operation in Ireland, with excellent results, for over a half-century. It has, also, been in operation for several years in the Catholic schools of Nova Scotia. It has been introduced in not a few places in the United States, as a temporary and local adjustment of the difficulties of the school question, and, wherever it has been tried, no cause is found for complaint. The Jesuit Fathers seem to have been its first patrons in the United States. They had for a long time schools under this plan in Florissant, Missouri, and in Conewago, Pennsylvania, and still have several schools under the same plan in New Mexico. This plan is sometimes called "the Poughkeepsie plan," having been in operation for a long time with great success in Poughkeepsie, New York; sometimes also "the Georgia plan" having been introduced on a rather extensive scale into the Catholic schools of Georgia through the influence of the late Cardinal Persico while he was Bishop of Savannah.

edifice which Americans have reared in their devotion to education would Catholics remove or permit to be removed. They would fain add to its splendor and majesty by putting side by side religious and secular instruction, neither of them interfering with the other, each of them borrowing from the other aid and dignity. Do the schools of America fear contact with religion? Catholics demand the Christian state school. In so doing, they prove themselves truest friends of the school and of the state.*

* It must be confessed that the American people view with but little favor any measure to impart religious instruction in connection with state schools, and the problem of the moral and religious instruction of the masses of the people still remains to be faced.

John Ireland:
Clarification to Cardinal Gibbons*
(1890)

Ireland's address to the National Educational Association became an immediate target of criticism. The sharpest arrows came from several of his brother bishops, most notably, Bishop Bernard J. McQuaid of Rochester, close friend and adviser of another formidable critic, Archbishop Michael A. Corrigan of New York. These two men, along with the "German" bishops of the Midwest, represented the conservative leadership of the American Church. To them, the suggestion of voluntarily abandoning the parish schools, which had taken decades to build and staff, was simply suicidal. When serious complaints were lodged in Rome, Pope Leo XIII asked Cardinal Gibbons for his opinion on the issue. Actually, Gibbons had studied the speech and approved of it. He favored the compromise approach wherever local circumstances dictated it and so offered in St. Paul a spirited defense of his long-time friend. The following letter from Ireland supplied him with necessary background.

* "Archbishop Ireland's Letter to Cardinal Gibbons Explaining in Detail His Address on State Schools at St. Paul in July, 1890," in Daniel F. Reilly, *The School Controversy (1891–1893)* (Washington, D.C.: The Catholic University of America Press, 1943), Appendix B, pp. 237–241.

YOUR EMINENCE,

I beg leave to pen down a few lines, with the intent of making somewhat clear the meaning of my address on "Schools."

I am free to say that it is difficult for me to see anything in it calling for or deserving censure. I have read all the objections raised against it in German papers, and my judgment is that those objections arise from malice prepense in wresting certain phrases from the context, and giving to them an interpretation which antecedent and subsequent declarations do not permit. It is possible, too, that they are in some degree due to ignorance of the true ethical principles which underlie the school question, and to the dislike which so many Catholics entertain for American institutions, or American ideas. I cannot bring myself to believe that those in Rome, finding fault with me, could have had my whole discourse before their eyes: garbled extracts were sent to them, & from these their judgment is formed. My best defense is a perusal of the whole discourse.

The general purpose of the discourse was to state plainly to the country the grounds of Catholic opposition to the State Schools, & to lead up, if possible, to an alteration permitting the removal of this opposition. I was anxious, too, incidentally to allay the angry feeling which reigns between non-Catholic Americans & Catholics, in so far as this feeling rests on misunderstanding of our position. These misunderstandings derive fully as much from exaggerations and misstatements made by Catholics as from ill will or prejudice on the part of non-Catholics.

I had a grand opportunity opened to me; the country was my audience.

The impression is abroad that the Church is opposed

to State Schools and to State interference in education, because she is opposed to the education of the children of the people. I desire to set her right before the country on these points.

I admitted in principle the State School—Thus the State, I said, has the right to establish & maintain Schools. Instruction being so necessary in America for good citizenship, and the means of instruction being beyond the reach of many children, thro' poverty or ill will of parents, I asserted the duty on the part of the State, to maintain Schools, in which all children, the poorest & the most abandoned, would be instructed. Of course, in this point, I am dealing with abstract right & duty: in the concrete, as my whole discourse plainly shows, I require that this right be so exercised that while the State obtain its purposes, the purposes of the Church be not frustrated.

I upheld compulsory education, & in this I have with me numerous Catholic writers, Rickaby,* Bouquillon,† etc. German papers raise a great clamor against me on this point as if I denied to parents that right to control the education of their children. Well, I am most plain & strong in declaring that this right belongs primarily to the parents, and that the State has no right to give itself instruction except when parents neglect their duty. Nor do I allow the State to demand attendance in its own Schools—except when parents neglect absolutely

---

* Joseph Rickaby (1845–1932), an English Jesuit, was a prominent writer on philosophical and theological subjects. Ireland regarded the Jesuits as a group as his greatest adversaries on the "school question."—N. G. McC.

† Thomas Bouquillon (1840–1902), a Belgian-born theologian at the Catholic University of America. His pamphlet *Education: To Whom Does It Belong?* (Baltimore: John Murphy & Co., 1891) challenged the traditional view that the State has only a substitutional right in education.—N. G. McC.

their children. Abundant room is left for home schools, parish schools, etc. Bishop Katzer* took publicly the position that the State must enact no school-law, erect no school-building, that the parent had the right, if he desired, to bring up his child in ignorance, total ignorance. Of course, he thinks me heretical.

"Free Schools! Blessed indeed is the nation whose vales and hill sides they adorn, and blessed the generations upon whose souls are poured their treasures!"

A fearful cry went out against those words, as if I extolled the present free-schools of America as being perfect. Well, it is clear that I am talking of free schools in the abstract—free instruction, to be had by all for the asking. Later on, I will show emphatically what free schools in the concrete must be—schools in which religion is taught.

"It were idle for me to praise the State-School of America in the *imparting of secular instruction*. It is our pride and our glory." German papers have kept for weeks a garbled version of these words in large headlines, actually cutting the sentence in twain, so as to take out of it my meaning. "It were idle for me to praise the State School of America. It is our pride and our glory"—So they wrote. I restricted my praise to the "imparting of secular instruction," and in this matter who will contradict me?

I granted to the State School its full quota of merit, so that my censure of it might not seem to come from prejudice. And that censure came—clear and unmistakable. How men—priests—bishops could write that I endorsed the public-school, passes my understanding. I said: "Can I be suspected of enmity to the State School—

* Frederick F. X. Katzer (1844–1903), Bishop of Green Bay from 1886 to 1891, became Archbishop of Milwaukee in 1891.—N. G. McC.

because I tell of defects which I seek to remedy? . . . There is dissatisfaction with the State School as at present organized."—and I consecrate two-thirds of the discourse to give the grounds of this dissatisfaction. I add "the dissatisfaction will exist as long as no change is made. It is founded on conscience."

"The free Schools of America! Withered be the hand raised in sign of their destruction!"—Another sentence for which I was threatened with excommunication. My meaning was that I would not destroy, but improve, correct, enlarge. "I fain would widen the expanse of their wings until all the children of the people find shelter beneath their cover—" "Not one stone of the wondrous edifice which Americans have built up in their devotion to education will Catholics remove, or permit to be removed. They would fain add to its splendor and majesty by putting side by side religion and the School"—I was addressing Protestants, the born defenders of the schools —teachers. What was I to do to gain their ear, but to confess to all the good in the system, and, then, when their sympathy is won, to tell of the defects!

"I turn to the parish school. It exists. I repeat my regret that there is the necessity for its existence. In behalf of the State School I call upon my fellow Americans to aid in the removal of this necessity." On this point Father Abbelen* of Milwaukee has raised a dreadful clamor in Milwaukee papers; German and English priests of Wisconsin replied to him.

I cannot but think I am right and that Abbelen is wrong. Be it understood that I always allow the right of a parish to have a parish school, no matter how perfect

---

* Peter M. Abbelen (1843–1917), Vicar-General of the Archdiocese of Milwaukee, was a leader in the effort to have German-language parishes established wherever there were immigrants.—N. G. McC.

the state school may be. But my contention is that the state school, rightly organized—sustained by State funds, and yet granting to Catholic children all that is needed for the protection of the State, no absolute necessity exists for the parish school. In Ireland [and] England there is no strictly-speaking parish school. In Belgium and France, no parish-school was thought of until infidel governments had made the State school infidel. The necessity for parish-schools is hypothetical—the necessity being not a direct result of the Church's mission, but a provision in certain cases for the protection of the faith. The Church is not established to teach writing and ciphering, but to teach morals and faith, and she teaches writing and ciphering only when otherwise morals and faith could not be taught. Abbelen makes out that the "Docete gentes" implies teaching all that children have to learn—quod est absurdum.

Now, what is required in the State-School to make it acceptable to us, I develop in two-thirds of my discourse. I am sure you will find this part ultra abstract. I demand positive Catholic dogmatic teaching—rejecting mere moral teaching, rejecting totally the so-called "common Christianity" theory. Now, my opponents pass over in absolute silence this part of the discourse, which is the more important part, which secular papers took to be properly the discourse.

One point here has been criticized. It is this: "I am a Catholic, of course, to the tiniest fibre of my heart, unflinching and uncompromising in my faith. But God forbid that I desire to see in America the ground which protestantism occupies exposed to the chilling and devastating blast of unbelief. Let me be your ally in stemming the swelling tide of irreligion."—Why, said one priest in a German paper, Abp. Ireland has lost the faith: he is willing to keep up Protestantism. Of course, my meaning is that of words, spoken by Manning and Newman—that factional Christianity is better than materialism. Besides I took the standpoint of your Eminence's book—of speaking to Americans in the name of our "Christian Heritage"—and in this name asking them to make the Schools Christian—Catholic for us, and Protestant for themselves. We cannot have Catholic State Schools without giving them Protestant State Schools.

My appeal for State Schools fit for Catholic children has been censured under the plea that a Protestant state should touch nothing Catholic. But America is not a "Protestant State," and if Catholics pay school taxes they should receive benefit from them. The burden upon our Catholics to maintain parish schools up to the required standard for all the children of the Church is almost unbearable. There is danger that never shall we have schools for all Catholic children, or that Catholics will grow tired of contributing. At present nearly half the Catholic children of America do not attend parish-schools. The true solution, in my judgment, is to make the State-School satisfactory to Catholic consciences, and to use it. Can this be done? Let us try. If it cannot be done, let us do our best with our parish-schools.

Besides have not bishops and priests gone too far in their denunciations of the State School? Have they not, in their desire to protect the parish school, often belied, in their exaggerations of the evil, the State School? Have they not gone beyond the "Apostolic Instruction" of 1875? Have they not needlessly brought upon us the odium of the country? Indeed, since our own schools are neither numerous enough, nor efficient enough for our

children, and many of these must attend the public
school, have we not done immense harm to souls by our
anathemas? Catholics in many cases must use those
schools, and yet they are denounced for it; their consciences are falsified—they are estranged from the
Church. I am not afraid to say that in places where
bishops have been very severe against Public schools,
their parish schools have done more harm than good to
religion.

It is well, too, to remark that our public schools, in
many places at least, are not *positively* bad. They are
not *hot beds* of vice; neither do they teach unbelief or
Protestantism. Teachers are often good Catholics; or at
least they are gentlemen or ladies, decorous in conduct,
and generous toward our faith. I know well the immense
advantage to children of positive dogmatic teaching in
school; yet, where the school is as nearly neutral as can
be—the family and the Sunday School can do much—
tho' never all we should give if circumstances permit.

Our public-schools are better than those of France and
Italy, and in those countries we hear no continuous
anathemas.

At any rate, continuous anathemas only irritate. Ger-
mans have actually said I was disloyal to the Church
when I did not stand up before the Convention and tell
of the immoralities and the scepticism of the public-
schools.

Now, as to my remedies for bringing together State and
Church. Those remedies of mine were put forth tenta-
tively, and as mere beginnings. We cannot have all at
once; let us get an entering wedge. The system of pay-
ment by results is the system of England—to which Catholics gladly subscribe. The "Poughkeepsie Plan" is the

Irish System in vogue for 40 years—used by sisters and brothers—with the sole exception of the Christian brothers. In this system teachers and pupils are all Catholics; the atmosphere is Catholic; all secular teaching is from Catholic minds and from Catholic hearts. The one point is, that positive dogmatic teaching is before or after legal school-hours. Catechism, it is said, should be free at all hours: what does it matter whether it be taught at nine A.M. or eleven A.M.! It is not, as a fact, taught at all hours. But the crucifix is to be removed: Abp. Ireland is the enemy of the crucifix. But the crucifix often is not in Catholic schools, and religion is not dependent on one symbol. Nor is the atmosphere neutral: It cannot be neutral while teachers and pupils are Catholic.

I have myself no further remarks to make. If fault were to be found in Rome with the address, let the precise point with which fault is found be quickly pointed out to me and I will give explanation, or if necessary quietly withdraw it. A public condemnation from Rome of the address would set America in fury, as it would be a direct attack on principles which America will not give up, that is the right of the State to provide for the instruction of all children. As I am so clear on the need of religion in the Schools, Rome's condemnation will be understood to bear on the fact that I allow any right to the State.

I repeat—I have read all the objections to the discourse, and they come either from partial reading of my words, or from hatred of the American state.

The "Poughkeepsie Plan" is in existence in very many of our Catholic country settlements, with the best possible results. Sisters teach, and without the aid of state

funds, Sisters could not be supported in those settlements. Had I made the effort, I could have had it in
St. Paul. But this war made on me disturbs me.

I will write you again tomorrow. Meanwhile, I repeat
my expression of deep gratitude and sincere affection,
and remain,

Very respectfully,

JOHN IRELAND

8. Archbishop Satolli's Fourteen Propositions for the Settling of the School Question* (1892)

The press, both secular and Catholic, devoted great attention to what came to be called simply the "school question." Could Catholics co-operate with the system of public education along the lines of the Poughkeepsie Plan in New York or the Faribault-Stillwater Plan in Minnesota? Rome's answer came in May 1892: "The sound decrees of the Baltimore Council as to parochial schools remaining fully in force, the agreement made by the Most Rev. Dr. John Ireland with regard to the Faribault and Stillwater schools, all the circumstances being taken into consideration, can be allowed." Instead of settling the issue, both sides argued that Rome had ruled in their favor. Did the Latin phrase tolerari potest *mean toleration, permission, or approval?† The press*

* "Archbishop Francis Satolli's Fourteen Propositions Presented November 17, 1892, to the Archbishops of the United States for the Settling of the School Question," in Daniel F. Reilly, *The School Controversy (1891–1893)* (Washington, D.C.: The Catholic University of America Press, 1943), Appendix G, pp. 271–276.

† Archbishop Corrigan publicly announced that the Faribault system had been condemned, and only the special case tolerated. Following this, his already low stock in the Midwest plummeted out of sight. This excerpt from the *Chicago Post* of May 12, 1892, captures some of the color of the battle, as it waxed in the public press: "These differences of opinion between two bishops of the Roman

kept the pot boiling noisily; relations between the two camps became even more strained. In November, the pope sent a personal legate, Archbishop Francis Satolli, to the meeting of the American archbishops with this set of proposals for resolving the controversy finally.

I

All care must be taken to erect Catholic schools, to enlarge and improve those already established, and to make them equal to the public schools in teaching and in discipline. (Conc. Plen. Balt. III, No. 197, p. 101.)

II

When there is no Catholic school at all, or when the one that is available is little fitted for giving the children an education in keeping with their condition, then the public school may be attended with a safe conscience, the danger of perversion being rendered remote by opportune remedial and precautionary measures, a matter that is to be left to the conscience and judgment of the ordinaries. (*Ibid.*, No. 198, p. 103.)

Catholic hierarchy are, we think, of the smallest possible consequence to the cause of popular education in America; because whatever the merits or demerits of the Faribault plan, from the Roman point of view, it is a plan which is most unlikely to obtain considerable vogue in this country. It is agreeable to neither Roman or anti-Roman religionists. The debate has simply afforded an opportunity to the Archbishop of New York to exhibit anew the qualities which distinguish him as the most narrow, dictatorial, truculent and deservedly unpopular Roman Catholic prelate in America. . . . The controversy has left John Ireland, on the other hand, in the position he has long held, as at once a patriot and churchman of the first rank."

III

We enact and command that no one shall be allowed to teach in a parochial school who has not proven his fitness for the position by previous examination. No priest shall have the right to employ any teacher, male or female, in his school without a certificate of ability or a diploma from the diocesan board of examiners. (*Ibid.*, No. 203, p. 108.)

IV

Normal schools, as they are called, are to be established where they are wanted and are evidently necessary. (*Ibid.*, No. 205, p. 110.)

V

We strictly forbid any one, whether bishop or priest,— and this is the express prohibition of the Sovereign Pontiff through the Sacred Congregation,—either by act or by threat, to exclude from the sacraments, as unworthy, parents who choose to send their children to the public schools. As regards the children themselves, this enactment applies with still greater force. (*Ibid.*, No. 198, p. 104; cf. Tit. VI, Cap. I, II; Tit. VII.)

VI

To the Catholic Church belongs the duty and the divine right of teaching all nations to believe the truth of the Gospel, and to observe whatsoever Christ commanded (Matth. xxviii, 19); in her, likewise, is vested the divine right of instructing the young, in so far as theirs is the kingdom of Heaven (Mark, x, 14; conf.

Conc. Balt. Pl. III., No. 194); that is to say, she holds for herself the right of teaching the truths of faith and the law of morals in order to bring up youth in the habits of a Christian life. Hence, absolutely and universally speaking, there is no repugnance in their learning the first elements and the higher branches of arts and the natural sciences in public schools, controlled by the state, whose office it is to provide, maintain, and protect everything, by which its citizens are formed to moral goodness, while they live peaceably together, with a sufficiency of temporal goods, under laws promulgated by civil authority.

For the rest, the provisions of the Council of Baltimore are yet in force and, in a general way, will remain so; to wit: "Not only out of our paternal love do we exhort Catholic parents, but we command them, by all the authority we possess, to procure a truly Christian and Catholic education for the beloved offspring given them of God, born again in baptism unto Christ and destined for Heaven, to shield and secure them throughout childhood and youth from the dangers of a merely worldly education, and, therefore, to send them to parochial or other truly Catholic schools." United with this duty are the rights of parents, which no civil law or authority can violate or weaken.

VII

The Catholic Church, in general, and especially the Holy See, far from condemning or treating with indifference the public schools, desires rather that, by the joint action of civil and ecclesiastical authorities, there should be public schools in every State, according as the circumstances of the people require, for the cultivation of the useful arts and natural sciences; but the Catholic Church shrinks from those features of public schools which are opposed to the truths of Christianity and to morality, and since, in the interest of society itself, these objectionable features are removable, therefore not only the bishops, but the citizens at large should labor to remove them, in virtue of their own right and in the cause of morality.

VIII

It is long since the Holy See, after consultation with the Bishops of the United States of America, decreed that parish schools and other institutions, under the direction of the bishop, each according to the conditions of its own diocese, were opportune and necessary for Catholic youth, from the fact that it was held for certain that the public schools bore, within themselves, a proximate danger to faith and morals for various reasons (Conc. Balt. III., No. 194 seq.; App. p. 279); viz., because a purely secular education is given in the public school— inasmuch as it excludes all teaching of religion—because teachers are chosen indiscriminately from every sect, and no law prevents them from working the ruin of youth— so that they are at liberty to instill errors and the germs of vice in tender minds. Likewise, certain corruption seemed to impend from the fact that in these schools, or at least in many of them, children of both sexes are brought together for their lessons in the same room.

Wherefore, if it be clear that, in a given locality, owing to the wiser dispositions of public authorities, or the watchful prudence of school board, teachers, and parents, the above named dangers to faith and morals disappear, then it is lawful for Catholic parents to send their chil-

dren to these schools, to acquire the elements of letters
and arts, provided the parents themselves do not neglect
their most serious duty, and the pastors of souls put
forth every effort to instruct the children and train them
in all that pertains to Catholic worship and life.

IX

It is left to the judgment and the wisdom of the Ordinaries to decide whether, in a certain part of their
respective dioceses, a parochial school can be built and
kept up in a fitting condition, not inferior to the public
schools, taking in consideration the temporal conditions
of the parents, while graver needs for procuring their
spiritual welfare and the decent support of the Church
are pressing. It will be well, therefore, as was the wont
of our forefathers, and as was done in the early days of
the Church, to establish weekly classes of catechism,
which all the children of the parish should attend; for
the better success of this measure, let the zeal of pastors
in fulfilling their duty and the love of Catholic parents
leave no effort unspared. (Cf. Conc. Pl. Balt. III, No.
198.)

X

No reproach, either in public or in private, shall be cast
upon Catholic parents who send their children to private
schools or academies, where a better education is given
under the direction of religious or of approved and
Catholic persons. If they make sufficient provision for
the religious training of their children, let them be free
to secure, in other ways, that education, which the position of their family requires.

XI

It is greatly to be desired and will be a most happy arrangement, if the bishop agree with the civil authorities, or with the members of the school board, to conduct the school with mutual attention and due consideration for their respective rights.

While there are teachers of any description for the secular branches, who are legally inhibited from offending Catholic religion and morality, let obtain the right and duty of the Church to teach the children catechism, in order to remove dangers to their faith and morals from any quarter whatsoever.

. . .

XII

As for those Catholic children that, in great numbers, are educated in the public schools, where now, not without danger, they receive no religious instruction at all, strenuous efforts should be made not to leave them without sufficient and seasonable instruction in Catholic faith and practice. We know, by experience, that not all our Catholic children are found in our Catholic schools. Statistics show that hundreds of thousands of Catholic children, in the United States of America, attend schools which are under the control of State boards, and in which, for that reason, teachers of every denomination are engaged. Beyond all doubt, the one thing necessary, *i.e.,* religious and moral education, according to Catholic principles, is not to be treated either lightly or with delay, but, on the contrary, with all earnestness and energy.

The adoption of one of three plans is recommended,

the choice to be made according to local circumstances in the different States and various personal relations.

The first consists in an agreement between the bishop and members of the school board, whereby they, in a spirit of fairness and good will, allow the Catholic children to be assembled, during free time, and taught catechism; it would also be of the greatest advantage if this plan were not confined to the primary schools, but were extended, likewise, to the high schools and colleges, in the form of a free lecture.

The second: To have a catechism class outside the public school building and also classes of higher Christian Doctrine, where, at fixed times, the Catholic children would assemble with diligence and pleasure, induced thereto by the authority of their parents, the persuasion of their pastors, and the hope of praise and rewards.

The third plan does not seem, at first sight, so suitable, but it is bound up more intimately with the duty of both parents and pastors. Pastors should unceasingly urge upon parents that most important duty, imposed both by natural and divine law, of bringing up their children in sound morality and Catholic faith. Besides, the instruction of children appertains to the very essence of the pastoral charge: let the pastor of souls say to them with the Apostle: "My little children of whom I am in labor again until Christ be formed in you (Gal., iv, 19)." Let him have classes of children in the parish, such as have been established in Rome and in many other places, and even in churches in this country, with very happy results.

Nor let him, with little prudence, show less love for the children that attend the public schools than for those that attend the parochial schools; on the contrary, stronger marks of loving solicitude are to be shown them; the Sunday school and the hour for catechism should be devoted to them in a special manner. And to cultivate this field, let the pastor call to his aid other priests, religious, and even suitable members of the laity, in order that what is supremely necessary be wanting to no child.

XIII

For the standing and growth of Catholic schools, it seems that care should be taken that the teachers prove themselves qualified, not only by previous examination before the diocesan board, and by certificate, or diploma, received from it, but also by having a teacher's diploma from the school board of the State, awarded after successful examination. This is urged, first, so as not to appear regardless, without reason, of what public authority requires for teaching. Secondly, a better opinion of Catholic schools will be created. Thirdly, greater assurance will be given to parents that, in Catholic schools, there is no deficiency to render them inferior to public schools; that, on the contrary, everything is done to make Catholic schools equal to public schools, or even superior. Fourthly, and lastly we think that this plan would prepare the way for the State to see, along with the recognized and tested fitness of the teachers, that the laws are observed in all matter pertaining to the arts and sciences, to method and pedagogics, and to whatever is ordinarily required to promote the stability and usefulness of the schools.

XIV

It is necessary that what are called normal schools should reach such efficiency in preparing teachers of letters, arts, and sciences that their graduates shall not fail to obtain the diploma of the State. For the sake of the Catholic cause, let there be among laymen a growing rivalry to take the diploma and doctorate, so that, possessed of knowledge and qualifications requisite for teaching, they may compete for and honorably obtain positions in the public high schools, colleges, and scientific institutions.

The knowledge of truth of every kind, straightforward justice united with charity, the effulgence and appreciation of the liberal arts—these are the bulwarks of the Church.

All the above was read and considered in the meeting of the Archbishops, the difficulties answered, and the requisite alterations made, November 17, 1892.

9. Bishop McQuaid's Letter to Pope Leo XIII on the School Question*
(1892)

The Fourteen Propositions of Archbishop Satolli distressed some of the bishops, who thought they would weaken, and perhaps destroy, the parochial school system. The Bishop of Louisville wrote to Archbishop Corrigan that the Propositions would be "the death blow, to a certain extent, of our Catholic schools."† As could be expected, the Bishop of Rochester was thoroughly aroused. To Corrigan he wrote: "We are all in a nice pickle, thanks to Leo XIII and his delegate. Just as our arduous work of the last forty years was beginning to bear ample fruit, they arbitrarily upset the whole. If an enemy had done this! It is only a question of time, when present Roman legislation having wrought incalculable mischief, that we, school-children of the hierarchy, will again receive a lesson in our Catechism from another Italian sent out to enlighten us."‡ In more discreet fashion he wrote to the pope, commenting unfavorably on nine of the Propositions.

* McQuaid to Leo XIII, Rochester, December 13, 1892, in F. J. Zwierlein, *The Life and Letters of Bishop McQuaid* (Rochester, N. Y.: The Art Print Shop, 1927), III, 191–193, 196.

† Zwierlein, *op. cit.*, III, 187.

‡ *Ibid.*

I thank your Holiness for the opportunity given me to write upon a subject that gravely concerns the spiritual welfare of our Catholic people in the United States, and about which their minds and souls are at present greatly disturbed.

After the Third Plenary Council of Baltimore we had peace in the Church and all, bishops, priests, and people, seemed intent on promoting the establishment of Catholic schools as rapidly as possible. The first note of alarm came from a dangerous address delivered at St. Paul before a Convention of State Schoolteachers. This address of Archbishop Ireland pained and bewildered all who had followed carefully the school question as it has been discussed in America. Already many efforts had been made to effect a compromise with the State on a basis that would protect the faith and morals of our Catholic children. These efforts have invariably failed of adequate success. On such a basis as that of Faribault and Stillwater, actually put into effect in those towns, it would be easy in many places to bring about an adoption of our Catholic schools as State or public schools, but it would be by a complete sacrifice of the Catholic education and training of our children.

The only arrangement that is now possible between the State and Church on this question is one that entirely surrenders our rights, and that puts our schools on a par with the State schools from which the inculcation of morals based on religious motives is altogether excluded. Whenever the Catholic Church is ready to substitute the natural for the supernatural in religion the time will have arrived for passing over our schools to State control.

What we have most of all to dread is not the direct

teaching of the State schools, it is the indirect teaching which is the most insidious and the most dangerous. It is the moral atmosphere, the tone of thought permeating these schools that give cause for alarm. It is the indifferentism with regard to all religious beliefs we most of all fear. This is the dominant heresy that, imbibed in youth, can scarcely ever be eradicated. It is one that already has in our large towns and cities decimated Protestant churches. It is one that will decimate our churches if not checked in time. Indifferentism with regard to all religious ends is rank infidelity.

Associations in schools, especially in State schools, where all classes, Protestants, Jews and infidels, meet promiscuously, present another danger. In a State school all the children of these classes living within the school district are to be found. Watchful Christian parents would never allow their children to associate with such at other times, justly fearing contamination. Yet in State schools their children sit on the same benches with them, and meet them on the playground. Many Protestant parents refuse to send their children to State schools on account of this exposure, preferring private schools. Catholic children in attendance at Catholic schools frequent the Sacraments regularly, especially Penance, in which a safeguard is found for purity. When not in Catholic schools experience has shown that only a small number, and these of pious families, can be brought to confession. Other children, not Catholic, have no such protection for morality and esteem purity under a laxer system of intercourse between the sexes as less sacred. These associations, ripening into friendships, lead in time to mixed marriages, the growing evil of our time and country.

Experience has also demonstrated that Catholic chil-

dren brought up in State schools lose the spirit of the
Catholic religion; their thoughts and speech are tinc-
tured with a liberalism that borders on infidelity. A
common remark among this class is "All religions are
good enough or one religion is as good as another."

I speak with knowledge derived from an experience
of forty-five years in the priesthood in this my native
country, of which nearly twenty-five have been in the
episcopate. The maintenance of Catholic schools demands of bishops, priests and people great sacrifices,
much labor, and a large expenditure of money. I have
always believed that the cause of Catholic education was
worthy of such sacrifices. I believe it all the more strongly
now that I have read what your Holiness says to the
Italian people in the Encyclical of December 8.

For many years past I have felt that in this country
the Catholic school was as necessary for the children as
the Church was for them and their parents. For although
the chief mission of the Church is to preach the Gospel
of Christ, yet there is little likelihood of that Gospel
reaching and abiding in the hearts of the children except
through the instrumentality of the schoolhouse. Indeed
it will be useless to build churches that in one or two
generations hence will be vacant because children or
grandchildren of European parents no longer follow
the religion of their ancestors. If the Church in the
United States has already lost so many of her children,
it is due in large degree to the want of Catholic schools.

I also beg your Holiness to note that, in discussing the
question of State or Government in America, it is necessary to bear in mind that the State, in so far as it is an
executive body for the administration of the political
affairs of the country, is a creature of the people, and it
cannot go counter to the wishes and will of the people.

Hence until the people are educated up to a sense of rendering justice to their Catholic fellow-citizens in their schools, it is useless to appeal to what is called the State or Government. In certain localities people may be more intelligent and more just and better-disposed to admit our right to provide a Christian education for our children than in others. Just yet the people at large are not prepared to concede to us our just rights, while they are much more so than they were twenty or fifty years ago. The acceptance from them of anything less than our full rights, except as a temporary compromise, would be a misfortune for the Church in America. There should be no compromise at any time that sacrifices the right of our children to a Christian education.

.   .   .

I sum up by saying: (1). In a country like ours, whose form of government depends on the people, the less interference with our natural rights we concede to what is called the State the better. Later on, when our country becomes less Christian and more infidel, greater concessions will be demanded. All concessions in time acquire the force of rights. (2). Confessional, or denominational schools, such as they have in Canada and England, might answer in places where we cannot do better. (3). In my judgment, it may be generations before the American people will be disposed to listen to the adoption of confessional schools. (4). In the meantime our only alternative is to establish parochial schools wherever we can, and to raise the standard of secular education above that of the State schools, while not neglecting the religious care of these children who are obliged to go to the public schools because there are no parochial schools in their neighborhood. . . .

10.   John Lancaster Spalding:
"The Scope of Public-School Education"*
(1895)

*No Catholic leader of the last century commanded the
respect or wielded the influence of Bishop Spalding of
Peoria (1840–1916).† Descended from one of America's
oldest families, he was perhaps the best-educated and
most cultured prelate to grace the ranks of the hierarchy. In 1913, on the occasion of Spalding's golden
jubilee in the priesthood, Archbishop John J. Glennon
of St. Louis described him as "the one Catholic who
has best understood the American mind." His keen
intuition that America was the ideal habitat of the Catholic faith impressed Catholic and non-Catholic alike. He
had an appreciation of the function of public education
not shared by all his brethren in the hierarchy.*

* John Lancaster Spalding, *Means and Ends of Education*
(Chicago: A. C. McClurg & Co., 1895), pp. 140–150.

† "Few bishops had so great an influence on the life of the
people, even outside of religion and outside of the Catholic denomination, as had Bishop Spalding."—Pius X; quoted in Merle
Curti, *The Social Ideas of American Educators* (Paterson, N. J.:
Pageant Books, 1959), p. 348. "All serious and earnest-minded
thinkers engaged in solving the problems of education . . . have
received help from the personal counsels or from the educational
writings of the Bishop of Peoria."—William Torrey Harris; quoted
in Neil G. McCluskey, *Public Schools and Moral Education* (New
York: Columbia University Press, 1958), p. 169.

It is not possible for an enlightened mind not to take profound interest in our great system of public education. To do this he need not think it the best system. He may deem it defective in important requisites. He may hold, as I hold, that the system is of minor importance, the kind of teacher being all important. But if he loves his country, if he loves human excellence, if he has faith in man's capacity for growth, he cannot but turn his thoughts, with abiding attention and sympathy, to the generous and determined efforts of a powerful and vigorous people to educate themselves. Were our public-school system nothing more than the nation's profession of faith in the transforming power of education, it would be an omen of good and a ground for hope; and one cannot do more useful work than to help to form a public opinion which will accept with thankfulness the free play of all sincere minds about this great question, and which will cause the genuine lovers of our country to turn in contempt from the clamors politicians and bigots are apt to raise when an honest man utters honest thought on this all-important subject.

I am willing to assume and to accept as a fact that our theological differences make it impossible to introduce the teaching of any religious creed into the public school. I take the system as it is,—that is, as a system of secular education,—and I address myself more directly to the question proposed: What is or should be its scope?

The fact that religious instruction is excluded makes it all the more necessary that humanizing and ethical aims should be kept constantly in view. Whoever teaches in a public school should be profoundly convinced that man is more than an animal which may be taught cunning and quickness. A weed in blossom may have a certain beauty, but it will bear no fruit; and so the boy or youth one often meets, with his irreverent smartness, his precocious pseudo-knowledge of a hundred things, may excite a kind of interest, but he gives little promise of a noble future. The flower of his life is the blossom of the weed, which in its decay will poison the air, or, at the best, serve but to fertilize the soil. If we are to work to good purpose we must take our stand, with the great thinkers and educators, on the broad field of man's nature, and act in the light of the only true ideal of education,—that its end is wisdom, virtue, knowledge, power, reverence, faith, health, behavior, hope, and love; in a word, whatever powers and capacities make for intelligence, for conduct, for character, for completeness of life. Not for a moment should we permit ourselves to be deluded by the thought that because the teaching of religious creeds is excluded, therefore we may make no appeal to the fountainheads which sleep within every breast, the welling of whose waters alone has power to make us human. If we are forbidden to turn the current into this or that channel, we are not forbidden to recognize the universal truth that man lives by faith, hope, and love, by imagination and desire, and that it is precisely for this reason that he is educable. We move irresistibly in the lines of our real faith and desire, and the educator's great purpose is to help us to believe in what is high and to desire what is good. Since for the irreverent and vulgar spirit nothing is high or good, reverence, and the refinement which is the fruit of true intelligence, urge ceaselessly their claims on the teacher's attention. Goethe, I suppose, was little enough of a Christian to satisfy the demands of an agnostic cripple even, and yet he held that the best thing in man is the thrill of awe; and that the chief business of education is to cultivate reverence for whatever is above, beneath, around, and within us. This he believed to be the only philosophical and healthful attitude of mind and heart towards the universe, seen and unseen. May not the meanest flower that blows bring thoughts that lie too deep for tears? Is not reverence a part of all the sweetest and purest feelings which bind us to father and mother, to friends and home and country? Is it not the very bloom and fragrance, not only of the highest religious faith, but also of the best culture? Let the thrill of awe cease to vibrate, and you will have a world in which money is more than man, office better than honesty, and books like "Innocents Abroad" or "Peck's Bad Boy" more indicative of the kind of man we form than are the noblest works of genius. What is the great aim of the primary school, if it is not the nutrition of feeling? The child is weak in mind, weak in will, but he is most impressionable. Feeble in thought, he is strong in capacity to feel the emotions which are the sap of the tree of moral life. He responds quickly to the appeals of love, tenderness, and sympathy. He is alive to whatever is noble, heroic, and venerable. He desires the approbation of others, especially of those whom he believes to be true and high and pure. He has unquestioning faith, not only in God but in great men, who, for him, indeed, are earthly gods. Is not his father a divine man, whose mere word drives away all fear and fills him with confidence? The touch of his mother's hand stills his pain; if he is frightened, her voice is enough to soothe him to sleep. To imagine that we are educating this being of infinite sensibility and impressionability when we do little else than teach him to

read, write, and cipher, is to cherish a delusion. It is
not his destiny to become a reading, writing, and ciphering machine, but to become a man who believes, hopes,
and loves; who holds to sovereign truth, and is swayed by
sympathy; who looks up with reverence and awe to the
heavens, and hearkens with cheerful obedience to the
call of duty; who has habits of right thinking and well
doing which have become a law unto him, a second
nature. And if it be said that we all recognize this to be
so, but that it is not the business of the school to help to
form such a man; that it does its work when it sharpens
the wits, I will answer with the words of William von
Humboldt: "Whatever we wish to see introduced into
the life of a nation must first be introduced into its
schools."

Now, what we wish to see introduced into the life of
the nation is not the power of shrewd men, wholly ab-
sorbed in the striving for wealth, reckless of the means
by which it is gotten, and who, whether they succeed
or whether they fail, look upon money as the equivalent
of the best things man knows or has; who therefore think
that the highest purpose of government, as of other
social forces and institutions, is to make it easy for all
to get abundance of gold and to live in sloven plenty;
but what we wish to see introduced into the life of the
nation is the power of intelligence and virtue, of wisdom
and conduct. We believe, and in fact know, that humanity, justice, truthfulness, honesty, honor, fidelity,
courage, integrity, reverence, purity, and self-respect are
higher and mightier than anything mere sharpened wits
can accomplish. But if these virtues, which constitute
nearly the whole sum of man's strength and worth, are
to be introduced into the life of the nation, they must
be introduced into the schools, into the process of edu-

cation. We must recognize, not in theory alone but in practice, that the chief end of education is ethical, since conduct is three-fourths of human life. The aim must be to make men true in thought and word, pure in desire, faithful in act, upright in deed; men who understand that the highest good does not lie in the possession of anything whatsoever, but that it lies in power and quality of being; for whom what we are and not what we have is the guiding principle; who know that the best work is not that for which we receive most pay, but that which is most favorable to life, physical, moral, intellectual, and religious; since man does not exist for work or the Sabbath, but work and rest exist for him, that he may thrive and become more human and more divine. We must cease to tell boys and girls that education will enable them to get hold of the good things of which they believe the world to be full; we must make them realize rather that the best thing in the world is a noble man or woman, and to be that is the only certain way to a worthy and contented life. All talk about patriotism which implies that it is possible to be a patriot or a good citizen without being a true and good man, is sophistical and hollow. How shall he who cares not for his better self care for his country?

We must look, as educators, most closely to those sides of the national life where there is the greatest menace of ruin. It is plain that our besetting sin, as a people, is not intemperance or unchastity, but dishonesty. From the watering and manipulating of stocks to the adulteration of food and drink, from the booming of towns and lands to the selling of votes and the buying of office, from the halls of Congress to the policeman's beat, from the capitalist who controls trusts and syndicates to the mechanic who does inferior work, the taint of dishonesty is everywhere. We distrust one another, distrust those who manage public affairs, distrust our own fixed will to suffer the worst that may befall rather than cheat or steal or lie. Dishonesty hangs, like mephitic air, about our newspapers, our legislative assemblies, the municipal government of our towns and cities, about our churches even, since our religion itself seems to lack that highest kind of honesty, the downright and thorough sincerity which is its life-breath.

If the teacher in the public school may not insist that an honest man is the noblest work of God, he may teach at least that he who fails in honesty fails in the most essential quality of manhood, enters into warfare with the forces which have made him what he is, and which secure him the possession of what he holds dearer than himself, since he barters for it his self-respect; that the dishonest man is an anarchist and dissocialist, one who does what in him lies to destroy credit, and the sense of the sacredness of property, obedience to law, and belief in the rights of man. If our teachers are to work in the light of an ideal, if they are to have a conscious end in view, as all who strive intelligently must have, if they are to hold a principle which will give unity to their methods, they must seek it in the idea of morality, of conduct, which is three-fourths of life.

I myself am persuaded that the real and philosophical basis of morality is the being of God, a being absolute, infinite, unimaginable, inconceivable, of whom our highest and nearest thought is that he is not only almighty, but all-wise and all-good as well. But it is possible, I think, to cultivate the moral sense without directly and expressly assigning to it this philosophical and religious basis; for goodness is largely its own evidence, as virtue is its own reward. It all depends on the teacher. Life produces life, life develops life; and if the teacher have within himself a living sense of the all-importance of conduct, if he thoroughly realize that what we call knowledge is but a small part of man's life, his influence will nourish the feelings by which character is evolved. The germ of a moral idea is always an emotion, and that which impels to right action is the emotion rather than the idea. The teachings of the heart remain forever, and they are the most important; for what we love, genuinely believe in, and desire decides what we are and may become. Hence the true educator, even in giving technical instruction, strives not merely to make a workman, but to make also a man, whose being shall be touched to finer issues by spiritual powers, who shall be upheld by faith in the worth and sacredness of life, and in the education by which it is transformed, enriched, purified, and ennobled. He understands that an educated man, who, in the common acceptation of the phrase, is one who knows something, who knows many things, is, in truth, simply one who has acquired habits of right thinking and right doing. The culture which we wish to see prevail throughout our country is not learning and literary skill; it is character and intellectual openness,—that higher humanity which is latent within us all; which is power, wisdom, truth, goodness, love, sympathy, grace, and beauty; whose surpassing excellence the poor may know as well as the rich; whose charm the multitude may feel as well as the chosen few.

"He who speaks of the people," says Guicciardini, "speaks, in sooth, of a foolish animal, a prey to a thousand errors, a thousand confusions, without taste, without affection, without firmness." The scope of our public-school education is to make common-places of this kind, by which all literature is pervaded, so false as to be absurd; and when this end shall have been attained, Democracy will have won its noblest victory.

How shall we find the secret from which hope of such success will spring? By so forming and directing the power of public opinion, of national approval, and of money, as to make the best men and women willing and ready to enter the teacher's profession. The kind of man who educates is the test of the kind of education given, and there is properly no other test. When we Americans shall have learned to believe with all our hearts and with all the strength of irresistible conviction that a true educator is a more important, in every way a more useful, sort of man than a great railway king, or pork butcher, or captain of industry, or grain buyer, or stock manipulator, we shall have begun to make ourselves capable of perceiving the real scope of public-school education.

11. The Code of Canon Law on Catholic Education*
(1918)

The revised Code of Canon Law, the primary laws governing the universal Church, was promulgated in 1918. A canon (Greek: "a fixed rule or norm") is the most authoritative expression of the mind of the Church, embodying, as it generally does, generations of experience and wisdom. For the most part, the canons on education simply echo the assumptions and principles—in places, the actual wording—of the Instruction of Pius IX to the American bishops in 1875 (see pp. 121–126) and the legislation of the Third Council of Baltimore in 1884 (see pp. 93–94). The basic principle of parental responsibility for the child's education is stated in Canon 1113, part of the section on the sacrament of matrimony.† The Code treats in detail the Church's teaching authority in the fourth part of Book III.

Canon 1113. Parents are bound by a most serious obligation to provide to the best of their ability for the

* *Codex Juris Canonici* (Westminster, Md.: The Newman Press, 1949), pp. 374, 470–473. The text was translated by Neil G. McCluskey.

† A more detailed commentary on these canons may be found in Neil G. McCluskey, *Catholic Viewpoint on Education* (Garden City, N. Y.: Doubleday-Image, 1962), pp. 99–106.

religious and moral, as well as for the physical and civic, education of their children, and also to provide for their temporal welfare.

Canon 1372. 1. From childhood all the faithful must be brought up so that they are taught nothing contrary to faith and morals, but that religious and moral training have the primary place.

2. Not merely parents, as in Canon 1113, but all who take their place, possess the right and serious duty of providing a Christian education for their children.

Canon 1373. 1. In every elementary school religious instruction must be given suitable to the age of the children.

2. Young people in attendance at secondary schools or colleges must be given fuller instruction in religion, and let the bishops take care that this be done by priests conspicuous for zeal and learning.

Canon 1374. Catholic children may not attend non-Catholic, neutral, or mixed schools, that is, those which are open also to non-Catholics. It is for the local bishop to decide, in accordance with the instructions of the Holy See, under what circumstances and with what precautions against the danger of perversion, attendance at such schools may be allowed.

Canon 1375. The Church has the right to establish schools of every grade, not only elementary schools, but secondary schools and colleges.

Canon 1379. 1. Where there are no Catholic schools, as envisioned in Canon 1373, let provision be made for founding them, especially by the local bishops.

2. If the public universities are not imbued with Catholic doctrine and thought, it is desirable that a national or regional Catholic university be established.

3. The faithful must not neglect to lend their help, according to their means, for the establishment and support of Catholic schools.

Canon 1381. 1. The religious training of youth in all schools is subject to the authority and inspection of the Church.

2. The local bishops have the right and responsibility of watching out that nothing contrary to faith and morals be taught or take place in any schools within their territory.

3. Likewise, the bishops have the right to approve teachers of religion and religious textbooks; also, to demand the removal of either teachers or texts in the interests of religion and morality.

12.   Pastoral Letter
of the Archbishops and Bishops
of the United States*
(1919)

*So well had the Third Plenary Council done its work
that for thirty-five years the American Catholic community had ample guidelines for its continuing spectacular growth. The close of World War I and the grave
problems of social reconstruction left in its wake, however, were the occasion for the coming together of
bishops of the now one hundred dioceses for the first in a
series of what have since become annual meetings of the
hierarchy. Vision and courage stamp every page of the
fourteen sections of the pastoral. As a charter for social
action, this document has no peer in the literature of the
American Church. The first extract is from the introductory section, "Progress of the Church"; the second is
the entire Section XIII, "Education."*

The nursery of Christian life is the Catholic home; its
stronghold, the Catholic school. "In the great coming
combat between truth and error, between Faith and

* Peter Guilday, ed., *The National Pastorals of the American
Hierarchy, 1792–1919* (Washington, D.C.: National Catholic Welfare Council, 1923), pp. 280–284; 332–339.

Agnosticism, an important part of the fray must be borne by the laity. . . . And if, in the olden days of vassalage and serfdom, the Church honored every individual, no matter how humble his position, and labored to give him the enlightenment that would qualify him for higher responsibilities, much more now, in the era of popular rights and liberties, when every individual is an active and influential factor in the body politic, does she desire that all should be fitted by suitable training for an intelligent and conscientious discharge of the important duties that may devolve upon them."

The timely warning contained in these words from the Pastoral Letter of 1884, shows how clearly our predecessors discerned the need, both present and future, of Christian education. Their forecast has been verified. The combat which they predicted has swept around all the sources of thought, and has centered upon the school. There, especially, the interests of morality and religion are at stake; and there, more than anywhere else, the future of the nation is determined. For that reason, we give most hearty thanks to the Father of Lights who has blessed our Catholic schools and made them to prosper. We invoke His benediction upon the men and women who have consecrated their lives to the service of Christian education. They are wholesome examples of the self-forgetfulness which is necessary in time of peace no less than in crisis and danger. Through their singleness of purpose and their sacrifice, the Church expresses the truth that education is indeed a holy work, not merely a service to the individual and society, but a furtherance of God's design for man's salvation. With them we realize more fully than ever before, the necessity of adhering to the principles on which our schools are established. If our present situation is beset with new problems, it is also rich in opportunity; and we are confident that our teachers will exert themselves to the utmost in perfecting their work. Their united counsel in the Catholic Educational Association has already produced many excellent results, and it justifies the hope that our schools may be organized into a system that will combine the utilities of free initiative with the power of unified action. With a common purpose so great and so holy to guide them, and with a growing sense of solidarity, our educators will recognize the advantage which concerted effort implies both for the Catholic system as a whole and for each of the allied institutions.

We deem it necessary at this time to emphasize the value for our people of higher education, and the importance of providing and receiving it under Catholic auspices. "Would that even now, as we trust will surely come to pass in the future, the work of education were so ordered and established that Catholic youth might proceed from our Catholic elementary schools to Catholic schools of higher grade and in these attain the object of their desires."* This wish and ideal of our predecessors, in a gratifying measure, has been realized through the establishment of Catholic high schools and the development of our Catholic colleges. These have more than doubled in number; they have enlarged their facilities and adjusted their courses to modern requirements. We congratulate their directors and teachers, and with them we see in the present condition of their institutions, the possibility and the promise of further achievement in accordance with their own aspirations.

In educational progress, the teacher's qualification is

* Third Plenary Council: Acts and Decrees, 208.

the vital element. This is manifestly true of the Catholic school, in which the teacher's personality contributes so much toward the building of character and the preservation of faith along with the pupil's instruction in knowledge. If, therefore, the aim of our system is to have Catholic youth receive their education in its completeness from Catholic sources, it is equally important, and even more urgently necessary, that our teachers should be trained under those influences and by those agencies which place the Catholic religion at the heart of instruction, as the vitalizing principle of all knowledge and, in particular, of educational theory and practice. We note with satisfaction that our teachers are eager for such training, and that measures have been taken to provide it through institutes, summer schools and collegiate courses under university direction. We are convinced that this movement will invigorate our education and encourage our people, since the work of teachers who are thoroughly prepared is the best recommendation of the school.

We cannot too highly approve the zeal and liberality of those who, with large amount or small, have aided us in building up our schools. For what we value as significant in their action is not alone the material help which it renders, essential as this has become; but rather and chiefly the evidence which it affords of their spiritual sense and perception. It shows that they appreciate both the necessity of Catholic education and the unselfish devotion of our teachers. At a time, especially, when vast fortunes are so freely lavished upon education in other lines, it is edifying to see our people either dedicating their individual wealth to the cause of religious instruction or, as members of Catholic associations, combining their means for the same noble purpose. They, assuredly, have given an object lesson, teaching all by their example, "to do good, to be rich in good works, to give easily, to communicate to others, to lay up in store for themselves a good foundation against the time to come, that they may lay hold on the true life" (1 Timothy 6:18–19).

It was the progress of our academies, colleges and seminaries, from colonial days onward, that made the University possible; and it was the demand, created by them, for larger opportunities that made it a necessity. Established, at the instance of the Bishops, by Pope Leo XIII, it represents the joint action of the Holy See and of the American Hierarchy in behalf of higher education. Like the first universities of Europe, it was designed to be the home of all the sciences and the common base of all our educational forces. This twofold purpose has guided its development. As in the Ages of Faith and Enlightenment, the various Religious Orders gathered at the centers of learning which the Holy See had established, so in our own day, the Orders have grouped their houses of study about the University, in accordance with the express desire of its Founders. "We exhort you all," said the Pontiff, "to affiliate your seminaries, colleges and other Catholic institutions of learning with your University on the terms which its statutes suggest."* As the process of affiliation is extended to our high schools, it benefits them and also provides a better class of students for our colleges. In keeping, then, with the aims of its Founders, the University exists for the good and the service of all our schools. Through them and through their teachers, it returns with interest the generous support of our clergy and laity.

"By no means surprising or unexpected," said Pope

---

* Apostolic Letter, *Magni Nobis gaudii,* March 7, 1889.

Pius X, "is the steady and vigorous growth of the Catholic University which, located at Washington, the Capital City of the American Republic, built up by the offerings of the Catholic people and invested by the Apostolic See with full academic authority, is now become the fruitful parent of knowledge in all the sciences both human and divine. . . . We are fully determined on developing the Catholic University. For we clearly understand how much a Catholic university of high repute and influence can do toward spreading and upholding Catholic doctrine and furthering the cause of civilization. To protect it, therefore, and to quicken its growth, is, in Our judgment, equivalent to rendering most valuable service to religion and to country alike."*

To the same intent, Pope Benedict XV writes: "We have followed with joy its marvellous progress so closely related to the highest hope of your Churches . . . well knowing that you have all hitherto contributed in no small measure to the development of this seat of higher studies, both ecclesiastical and secular. Nor have we any doubt but that henceforth you will continue even more actively to support an institution of such great usefulness and promise as is the University."

It is our earnest desire that the University should attain fully the scope of its Founders, and thereby become an educational center worthy of the Church in America, worthy also of the zeal which our clergy and laity have shown in behalf of education. Its progress and prosperity will make it, as the Holy Father trusts, "the attractive center about which all will gather who love the teachings of our Catholic Faith."

•　　•　　•

* Letter to the Cardinal Chancellor, Jan. 5, 1912.

EDUCATION

The interests of order and peace require that our domestic, social and national relations be established on the solid basis of principle. For the attainment of this end, much can be done by wise legislation and by organized effort on the part of associations. We are confident that such effort and enactment will hasten the desired result. With their practical sense and their love of fairness, the American people understand that our national life cannot develop normally without adequate protection for the rights of all and faithful performance of duty by every citizen. And as they united to secure freedom for other nations, they now will strive together to realize their country's ideals.

Once more, however, we must emphasize the need of laying a sure foundation in the individual mind and conscience. Upon the integrity of each, upon his personal observance of justice and charity, depends the efficacy of legislation and of all endeavor for the common good. Our aim, therefore, should be, not to multiply laws and restrictions, but to develop such a spirit as will enable us to live in harmony under the simplest possible form, and only the necessary amount, of external regulation. Democracy, understood as self-government, implies that the people as a whole shall rule themselves. But if they are to rule wisely, each must begin by governing himself, by performing his duty no less than by maintaining his right.

Inasmuch as permanent peace on a sound basis is the desire of all our people, it is necessary to provide for the future by shaping the thought and guiding the purpose of our children and youth toward a complete understanding and discharge of their duties. Herein lies the importance of education and the responsibility of those to whom it is entrusted. Serious at all times, the educational problem is now graver and more complex by reason of the manifold demands that are made on the school, the changes in our industrial conditions, and above all, by reason of the confusion and error which obscure the purpose of life and therefore of true education.

Nevertheless, it is mainly through education that our country will accomplish its task and perpetuate its free institutions. Such is the conviction that inspires much of the activity displayed in this field, whether by individuals or by organizations. Their confidence is naturally strengthened by the interest which is taken in the school, the enlarged facilities for instruction and the increased efficiency of educational work.

But these again are so many reasons for insisting that education shall move in the right direction. The more thorough it becomes, the greater is its power either for good or for evil. A trained intelligence is but a highly tempered instrument, whose use must depend on the character of its possessor. Of itself knowledge gives no guarantee that it will issue in righteous action, and much less that it will redound to the benefit of society. As experience too plainly shows, culture of the highest order, with abundance of knowledge at its command, may be employed for criminal ends and be turned to the ruin of the very institutions which gave it support and protection. While, therefore, it is useful to improve education by organizing the work of the schools, enriching the content of knowledge and refining the methods of teaching, it is still more necessary to insure that all educational activity shall be guided by sound principles toward the attainment of its true purpose.

The Church in our country is obliged, for the sake of principle, to maintain a system of education distinct and separate from other systems. It is supported by the voluntary contributions of Catholics who, at the same time, contribute as required by law to the maintenance of the public schools. It engages in the service of education a body of teachers who consecrate their lives to this high calling; and it prepares, without expense to the State, a considerable number of Americans to live worthily as citizens of the Republic.

Our system is based on certain convictions that grow stronger as we observe the testing of all education, not simply by calm theoretic discussion, but by the crucial experience of recent events. It should not have required the pitiless searching of war to determine the value of any theory or system, but since that rude test has been so drastically applied and with such unmistakable results, we judge it opportune to restate the principles which serve as the basis of Catholic education.

First: The right of the child to receive education and the correlative duty of providing it, are established on the fact that man has a soul created by God and endowed with capacities which need to be developed for the good of the individual and the good of society. In its highest meaning therefore, education is a cooperation by human agencies with the Creator for the attainment of His purpose in regard to the individual who is to be educated, and in regard to the social order of which he is a member. Neither self-realization alone nor social service alone is the end of education, but rather these two in accordance with God's design, which gives to each of them its proportionate value. Hence it follows that education is essentially and inevitably a moral activity, in the sense that it undertakes to satisfy certain claims through the fulfilment of certain obligations. This is true independently of the manner and means which constitute the actual process; and it remains true, whether recognized or disregarded in educational practice, whether this practice include the teaching of morality, or exclude it, or try to maintain a neutral position.

Second: Since the child is endowed with physical, intellectual and moral capacities, all these must be developed harmoniously. An education that quickens the intelligence and enriches the mind with knowledge, but fails to develop the will and direct it to the practice of virtue, may produce scholars, but it cannot produce good men. The exclusion of moral training from the educative process is more dangerous in proportion to the thoroughness with which the intellectual powers are developed, because it gives the impression that morality is of little importance, and thus sends the pupil into life with a false idea which is not easily corrected.

Third: Since the duties we owe our Creator take precedence of all other duties, moral training must accord the first place to religion, that is, to the knowledge of God and His law, and must cultivate a spirit of obedience to His commands. The performance, sincere and complete, of religious duties, ensures the fulfilment of other obligations.

Fourth: Moral and religious training is most efficacious when it is joined with instruction in other kinds of knowledge. It should so permeate these that its influence will be felt in every circumstance of life, and be strengthened as the mind advances to a fuller acquaintance with nature and a riper experience with the realities of human existence.

Fifth: An education that unites intellectual, moral and religious elements, is the best training for citizenship. It inculcates a sense of responsibility, a respect for authority and a considerateness for the rights of others, which are the necessary foundations of civic virtue— more necessary where, as in a democracy, the citizen, enjoying a larger freedom, has a greater obligation to govern himself. We are convinced that, as religion and morality are essential to right living and to the public welfare, both should be included in the work of education.

There is reason to believe that this conviction is shared by a considerable number of our fellow-citizens who are not of the Catholic faith. They realize that the omission of religious instruction is a defect in education and also a detriment to religion. But in their view, the home and the church should give the needed training in morality and religion, leaving the school to provide only secular knowledge. Experience, however, confirms us in the belief that instead of dividing education among these several agencies, each of them should, in its own measure, contribute to the intellectual, moral and religious development of the child, and by this means become helpful to all the rest.

In order that the educative agencies may cooperate to the best effect, it is important to understand and safeguard their respective functions and rights. The office of the Church instituted by Christ is to "teach all nations," teaching them to observe whatsoever He commanded. This commission authorizes the Church to teach the truths of salvation to every human being, whether adult or child, rich or poor, private citizen or public official.

In the home with its limited sphere but intimate relations, the parent has both the right and the duty to educate his children; and he has both, not by any concession from an earthly power, but in virtue of a divine ordinance. Parenthood, because it means cooperation with God's design for the perpetuation of human kind, involves responsibility, and therefore implies a corresponding right to prepare for complete living those whom the parent brings into the world.

The school supplements and extends the educational function of the home. With its larger facilities and through the agency of teachers properly trained for the purpose, it accomplishes in a more effectual way the task of education, for which the parent, as a rule, has neither the time, the means nor the requisite qualifications. But the school cannot deprive the parent of his right nor absolve him from his duty, in the matter of educating his children. It may properly supply for certain deficiencies of the home in the way of physical training and cultivation of manners; and it must, by its discipline as well as by explicit instruction, imbue its pupils with habits of virtue. But it should not, through any of its administrations, lead the parent to believe that having placed his children in school, he is freed from responsibility, nor should it weaken the ties which attach the child to parent and home. On the contrary, the school should strengthen the home influence by developing in the child those traits of character which help to maintain the unity and happiness of family life. By this means it will cooperate effectually with the parent and worthily discharge its function.

Since the child is a member not only of the family but also of the larger social group, his education must prepare him to fulfil his obligations to society. The community has the right to insist that those who as members share in its benefits, shall possess the necessary qualifications. The school, therefore, whether private or public as regards maintenance and control, is an agency for social welfare, and as such it bears responsibility to the whole civic body.

While the social aspect of education is evidently important, it must be remembered that social righteousness depends upon individual morality. There are virtues, such as justice and charity, which are exercised in our relations with others; but there is no such thing as collective virtue which can be practiced by a community whose individual members do not possess it in any manner or degree. For this very reason, the attempt to develop the qualities of citizenship without regard for personal virtue, or to make civic utility the one standard of moral excellence, is doomed to failure. Integrity of life in each citizen is the only sure guarantee of worthy citizenship.

As the public welfare is largely dependent upon the intelligence of the citizen, the State has a vital concern in education. This is implied in the original purpose of our government which, as set forth in the preamble to the Constitution, is "to form a more perfect union, establish justice, ensure domestic tranquillity, provide for the common defense, promote the general welfare, and secure the blessings of liberty to ourselves and our posterity."

In accordance with these purposes, the State has a right to insist that its citizens shall be educated. It should encourage among the people such a love of learning that they will take the initiative and, without constraint, provide for the education of their children. Should they through negligence or lack of means fail to do so, the State has the right to establish schools and take every other legitimate means to safeguard its vital interests against the dangers that result from ignorance. In particular, it has both the right and the duty to exclude the teaching of doctrines which aim at the subversion of law and order and therefore at the destruction of the State itself.

The State is competent to do these things because its essential function is to promote the general welfare. But on the same principle, it is bound to respect and protect the rights of the citizen and especially of the parent. So long as these rights are properly exercised, to encroach upon them is not to further the general welfare but to put it in peril. If the function of government is to protect the liberty of the citizen, and if the aim of education is to prepare the individual for the rational use of his liberty, the State cannot rightfully or consistently make education a pretext for interfering with rights and liberties which the Creator, not the State, has conferred. Any advantage that might accrue even from a perfect system of State education, would be more than offset by the wrong which the violation of parental rights would involve.

In our country, government thus far has wisely refrained from placing any other than absolutely necessary restrictions upon private initiative. The result is seen in the development of our resources, the products of inventive genius and the magnitude of our enterprises. But our most valuable resources are the minds of our children; and for their development, at least the same scope should be allowed to individual effort as is secured to our undertakings in the material order.

The spirit of our people is in general adverse to State monopoly, and this for the obvious reason that such an absorption of control would mean the end of freedom and initiative. The same consequence is sure to follow when the State attempts to monopolize education; and the disaster will be greater inasmuch as it will affect, not simply the worldly interests of the citizen, but also his spiritual growth and salvation.

With great wisdom our American Constitution provides that every citizen shall be free to follow the dictates of his conscience in the matter of religious belief and observance. While the State gives no preference or advantage to any form of religion, its own best interests require that religion as well as education should flourish and exert its wholesome influence upon the lives of the people. And since education is so powerful an agency for the preservation of religion, equal freedom should be secured to both. This is the more needful where the State refuses religious instruction any place in its schools. To compel the attendance of all children at these schools, would be practically equivalent to an invasion of the rights of conscience, in respect of those parents who believe that religion forms a necessary part of education.

Our Catholic schools are not established and maintained with any idea of holding our children apart from the general body and spirit of American citizenship. They are simply the concrete form in which we exercise our rights as free citizens, in conformity with the dictates of conscience. Their very existence is a great moral fact in American life. For while they aim, openly and avowedly, to preserve our Catholic faith, they offer to all our people an example of the use of freedom for the advancement of morality and religion.

13. The American Hierarchy, "The Child: Citizen of Two Worlds"* (1950)

At the conclusion of the yearly week-long meeting of the hierarchy in Washington, D.C., it is customary to issue a formal statement touching some phase of church life, in the tradition of the pastoral letters that came out of the provincial and plenary councils of the nineteenth century. In 1950, the topic chosen for comment was the philosophy of Christian education. The statement is an impressive summary of that philosophy and merits thoughtful study by anyone wishing to know what the basis of education must be for a convinced Catholic. Here is the full text.

In the present grim international struggle, the American people have resolutely championed the cause of human freedom. We have committed ourselves to oppose relentlessly the aggressions of those who deny to man his God-given rights and who aim to enslave all mankind under the rules of Godless materialism. The responsibilities which we have thereby assumed are both grave and continuing. They deserve conscientious consideration.

* Raphael M. Huber, ed., *Our Bishops Speak* (Milwaukee, Wis.: The Bruce Publishing Co., 1952), pp. 161–169.

It is of primary importance for our people to realize that human freedom derives from the spiritual nature of man and can flourish only when things of the spirit are held in reverence. Our present principles of action need to be evaluated in the light of that truth. But we must go even further. Small comfort to be successful today if tomorrow the world finds us unworthy of the trust reposed in us. We need, therefore, to examine carefully what spiritual direction we are giving to our children to prepare them to fulfill their future moral responsibilities to God and to their fellow man.

In recent decades, striking advances have been made in meeting the child's physical, emotional, and social needs; but his moral and religious needs have not been met with the same solicitude and understanding. As a result, many of our children today betray confusion and insecurity because these unmet needs are fundamental to the harmonious development of their whole nature.

The child must be seen whole and entire. He must be seen as a citizen of two worlds. He belongs to this world surely, but his first and highest allegiance is to the kingdom of God. From his earliest years he must be taught that his chief significance comes from the fact that he is created by God and is destined for life with God in eternity.

The child's prospects for fulfilling this great hope which God has reposed in him must be viewed realistically. He will come to maturity in a society where social, moral, intellectual, and spiritual values are everywhere disintegrating. In such a society, he will urgently need the integrating force of religion as taught by Christ. Such a force will give him a complete and rational meaning for his existence.

First of all, it will arouse in him a consciousness of God

and of eternity. His vision will be opened out upon a supernatural world revealed by faith which differs from the world of nature his senses reveal. Thus he will discover a higher life than this daily one and a brighter world than he sees. Second, it will give him a continuing purpose in life, for it will teach him that he was made to know, love, and serve God in this world as the condition for meriting eternal happiness. Third, it will induce in him a deep sense of responsibility for those rights and obligations he possesses by reason of his citizenship in heaven as well as on earth. Finally, religion will challenge him to sanctify whatever walk of life he chooses and to seek and accept the will of God in whatever way it may be manifested. Thus, as a principle of integration, religion will help the child to develop a *sense of God,* a *sense of direction,* a *sense of responsibility,* and a *sense of mission* in this life.

I. SENSE OF GOD

The child is not complete in himself. He will find his completion only in life with God; and that life must begin here upon earth. Parents, therefore, should make early provision for their child's growth in God. This is not something to be postponed for nurture by school authorities. It must begin in the home through simple and prayerful practices. Morning and evening prayers, grace before and after meals, the family rosary, the saying of a short prayer each time the striking clock marks the passage of another hour nearer eternity, the reverential making of the Sign of the Cross, the inculcation of respect for the Crucifix and other religious objects—all these are practices which should be encouraged in the religious formation of the child. No one can doubt that there is a readiness on his part to receive such formation, and if parents are remiss in giving it they will lose a splendid opportunity to develop in their child that habitual awareness of God which is vital to his full growth.

Only two courses are open to the child—either he will be God-centered or self-centered. He is made and destined for God, but he bears in his nature the lingering effects of original sin which incline him to seek the satisfaction of every selfish whim. To correct this bend in his will so that God, rather than self, will occupy the center of his life is one of the most challenging tasks facing parents.

In meeting this challenge, let parents make use of the strong, supernatural motivation which can be drawn from the life of Christ. Let them encourage the imitation of Him, particularly in His obedience, patience, and thoughtfulness of others; and let them foster the emulation of that spirit of unselfish giving so characteristic of Christ. This can be done in many practical ways, particularly through providing the child with frequent opportunities for making acts of self-denial in the home. If he is taught to deny his selfish whims for the sake of Christ, he will not only discover a supernatural motive for his actions, but he will learn to give God that central place in his affections which God must occupy if the child is to come to his full spiritual stature.

Little point would be served in intensifying the child's awareness of God during his preschool years, if later his schooling were to rob him of that. The child's education during school years should be of a piece with his education at home. Catholic parents, clearly grasping this essential truth, have undergone great sacrifice and enormous expense to establish and maintain schools which will continue and enlarge the spiritual development of the child that was begun at home. In doing this, parents have acted within their competence, because it is they, and not the State, who possess the primary right to educate.

This natural right of parents is one which has ever been recognized in our American traditions. As recently as 1944, the highest court in our land confirmed it in these words: "It is cardinal with us that the custody, care, and nurture of the child *reside first in the parents* whose primary function and freedom include preparation for obligations the State can neither supply nor hinder."

In helping parents to exercise this right, the Church stands ready at hand with all her material and spiritual resources. At infancy she initiates the child into the life of grace and for the rest of his days she stands by his side ready to minister to his needs. She recognizes his preeminent need for God and she meets it by providing Catholic schools for each stage of his educational development. She does this in virtue of the sublime teaching office conferred upon her by Jesus Christ.

When it is impossible for parents to take advantage of the God-centered education which Catholic schools offer, they have a grave obligation to provide for their child's religious instruction in some other way. At least they must see that their children attend Catechism classes and vacation schools and receive the benefit of other activities of the Confraternity of Christian Doctrine.

Nor should the State, which has demonstrated a genuine interest in so many aspects of the child's welfare, be indifferent to the inherent value of religious instruction and training for the child attending tax-supported schools. The continuance and well-being of a State based on democratic principles require that it show a lively concern for moral principles and practices which are firmly grounded only in religion. For the child who is not receiving thorough religious education, the State should look with favor on released-time programs for his religious instruction.

Many important services have been rendered by governmental agencies to the child who has been deprived of the care and support of his parents by death, illness, or misfortune. However, it is a source of growing concern to us that in certain parts of our country there is a trend to regard this whole field of foster care as falling within the exclusive province of governmental authorities. It surely lies within their province to set up and enforce legitimate minimum standards of care for the dependent child; but the responsibility for his care should not be entirely assumed by them. There is a definite place in America for the voluntary agencies of mercy—particularly those operating under religious auspices, which are equipped to safeguard and develop the religious life of the dependent child. Certainly the child bereft of the immediate care of his parents is entitled to those opportunities for a religious upbringing, which his parents were obligated to give him. These opportunities can be best supplied by an agency operating under religious auspices.

II. SENSE OF DIRECTION

The child whose eyes have been opened to the vision of God must be encouraged to walk by the steady light of that vision; otherwise he will follow wandering fires. He is too young and immature to be left to himself. His impulses and desires, so largely unregulated because of his tender years, need to be given a sure direction by religious training, if he is to achieve that great purpose for which he was made: to know, to love, and to serve God.

The child must *know* God. There is a vast difference between "knowing about God" and "knowing God." The difference is made by personal experience. It is not enough that the child be given the necessary truths about God. They ought to be given in such a way that he will assimilate them and make them a part of himself. God must become as real to him as his own father or mother. God must not remain an abstraction. If He does, He will not be loved; and if He is not loved, then all the child's knowledge about Him will be sterile. Where love is, there too is service. "If you love me, keep my commandments." That is Christ's test and it must be applied to the child. He should be brought to see God's commandments and precepts as guideposts which give an unerring direction to his steps. In this work, the Church, the family and the school all have a part to play.

From the time that the Church pours the waters of Baptism over his forehead, until she surrenders him at death to God, there is no period when she does not provide the child, through her sacraments and teachings, with a steady inspiration to serve God. The inculcation of virtues, both natural and supernatural, the repeated warnings against succumbing to the demands of his lower nature, the balm with which she alleviates the wounds caused by sin in his life, and the channels of grace she holds constantly open for him—all these are aids which the Church gives the child in directing his steps toward God.

Parents are obligated to see that he makes ample use of these helps; and in addition they must inspire him to love and service of God by their own daily actions. The home will be his first school. He will be quick to imitate what he sees and hears there. Let them turn this impulse to imitate, which can be the source of much mischief and lasting harm, to the child's advantage by giving him at home a good example of Christian living.

If this example is not forthcoming, the child will become confused by the contradiction between what he is taught and what he sees practiced. This confusion will be compounded when he goes to a school where religion is taught. There he will be taught to reverence the name of God, but at home he will hear God's name used irreverently in petulance and anger. At school he will learn to co-operate and get along with his fellow pupils, but at home he will be allowed to offend and wrangle with his brothers and sisters. At school he will be taught strict precepts of honesty and justice, while at home he will hear his parents boast of sharp business practices and clever evasions of the truth. Disturbed by these contradictions and torn by conflicting loyalties to home and school, the child will lose confidence in his parents' and teachers' powers to give him effective direction.

A close association between home and school should be maintained by parents and school authorities so as to facilitate an exchange of views and confidences regarding the child. In this way, home and school life can be better integrated and there will be a reduction of those conflicts which very often are at work in his life, and which do not receive the understanding and attention they deserve.

When we speak of parents' responsibilities, it should be remembered that they do not devolve entirely upon the mother. The father has his responsibilities, too, and he must not shirk them. It is not enough for him to provide the material means of support for the family. He also has the obligation to identify himself with the interests and activities of his child. If the full benefits of parental direction are to be reaped by the child, such direction should include that steadying and stabilizing influence which it is the father's duty to exert.

Fathers and mothers have a natural competence to instruct their children with regard to sex. False modesty should not deter them from doing their duty in this regard. Sex is one of God's endowments. It should not be ignored or treated as something bad. If sex instruction is properly carried on in the home, a deep reverence will be developed in the child and he will be spared the shameful inferences which he often makes when he is left to himself to find out about sex. We protest in the strongest possible terms against the introduction of sex instruction into the schools. To be of benefit such instruction must be far broader than the imparting of information, and must be given individually. Sex is more than a biological function. It is bound up with the sacredness and uniqueness of the human personality. It can be fully and properly appreciated only within a religious and moral context. If treated otherwise, the child will see it apart from the controlling purpose of his life, which is service to God.

Many unsalutary influences are at work in modern society which must not be allowed free play upon the personality of the growing child. Parents should carefully regulate the company and the hours which their child keeps. They should not treat him as an adult. He needs to be warned against, even forbidden, certain associations. Particularly during adolescence, this is extremely important. A vigilant watch should be kept over the type of entertainment in which he indulges, the motion pictures he attends, the books he reads, the radio and television programs to which he is exposed in the home.

III. SENSE OF RESPONSIBILITY

A common complaint registered against the home and the school today is that they do not sharpen the child's sense of responsibility. He is made conscious of his rights, to be sure; but he also has obligations which are correlates of those rights. His education and training are defective in the proportion that those obligations are not impressed on his young mind.

No point is urged with greater insistency by religion than the accountability of each individual before God. It is the duty of parents to see to it that their child develops a deep sense of personal responsibility; learning at the earliest possible period that he is accountable to God for his thoughts, his words, and his actions. His home training must reinforce this teaching in every practical way. He should be held to strict account for the performance of chores and tasks which are given to him by his parents. He must be made to see that each member of the family has a part to play in the service of God by carrying out an assigned role. The child, thus enlightened, will be enabled to see in later life how the faithful discharge of his duties as a citizen can be related to the service of God.

Part of the boredom affecting our society today is due to the unsound separation which has developed between work and spiritual growth. The concept of work as a means of furthering sanctification has largely been lost. It remains for parents to recover that concept and apply it to the child's daily experience. From the consciousness that even the smallest household task when faithfully carried out draws him closer to God, the child will derive a continuing motivation for relating all that he does to God. And thus every task, no matter how trivial or menial, can take on a significance which will yield rich spiritual returns.

In this way the child will have learned at home a great lesson which will make it easier for him to adjust to the demands of school life. As he takes his place in that larger community, he will do so as a responsible individual. He will see his homework, his attention in class, and his participation in school activities as part of the same divine plan learned in the home, whereby each action has its significance in God's eyes. This mindfulness throughout his daily life of the supernatural value of his actions will be a safeguard against the careless performance of any duty. The greater his talent, the more he will be conscious of his obligation to serve God by a rightful exercise of that talent.

If the child is constantly aware that his time and his talents belong to God he will want to use them properly and will avoid those harmful associations and pastimes which frequently lead to juvenile delinquency. This implies however that adequate recreational facilities and opportunities for the development of his interest in hobbies, games and other activities are available so that his abounding energy can find wholesome channels for expression.

The spiritual helps which the child has for deepening his sense of responsibility must not be neglected. Parents should encourage the practice of nightly examination of conscience and weekly confession. The child who goes over his thoughts, speech, and actions at the end of each day, seeking out what has been displeasing to God, will gradually develop a sensitivity to God's claims upon his life. The practice of weekly confession will make him conscious of the manner in which he has misused his time and talents. It will heighten in him that sense of account-ability to God which is necessary if he is to show proper contrition for his failings and proper amendment of them.

IV. SENSE OF MISSION

In learning the valuable lesson that he is accountable to God for the use of his time and talents the child will acquire not only a sense of responsibility, but a sense of mission as well. For his religious training will remind him that his future happiness lies not in the indulgence of selfish desires, but in the complete dedication of his whole personality to God's service. "I am come to do the will of him who sent me." This must be the keynote of the child's mission in this world. For him the will of God must come to be more important than any personal consideration. Only when he masters this truth will he be given to see how all things, even disappointments and setbacks, can be turned to good account in the service of God.

Since everyone is not called to serve God in the same way or in the same capacity, great care should be ex-ercised in the child's vocational guidance. Otherwise, aimlessness in his training will leave him without perma-nent direction for his talents and aptitudes. Parents and teachers must help him to choose and to follow a calling for which he is fitted and in which he can best serve God. A deeper awareness in the child of his mission in life will do much to reduce the shocking waste of time and energy which in so many instances characterizes his formative years today, and later prevents him from taking his full place in civic life.

Among the boys and girls of our land, God has destined some to carry on the work of His Church for the salvation of souls. To these He has given a religious vocation. Here indeed is a challenge to the generosity of American parents. If in all sincerity they have impressed upon their child that he has a mission in life to do God's will, they in turn will want to co-operate with that will and aid in its fulfillment. God's claims are prior to every human consideration. If He calls the child to His special service, parents should not shrink from the sacrifice often entailed by such a call. The pain of severing home ties will be more than offset by the spiritual joy given to those who labor in the vineyard of the Lord.

In emphasizing the supreme importance of religion in the spiritual development of the child, we are but applying to the circumstances of today the eternal principles which the Church received from her divine Founder. For nineteen centuries, the Church has lingered lovingly over Christ's tribute to the child: "Suffer little children to come unto me and forbid them not; for of such is the kingdom of God." The implications of that tribute should be recognized by all who have care of the child. Theirs is the great vocation to show him that he is a citizen, not only of this world, but of that other world which lies beyond with God whose kingdom is the kingdom of children.

Neil G. McCluskey, S.J., Dean of the Faculties and Academic Vice President of Gonzaga University, was born in Seattle, Washington, in 1920. He received his B.A. and M.A. from Gonzaga University, his S.T.L. from Alma College, and his Ph.D. from Columbia University. After teaching philosophy and education at Seattle University, Father McCluskey served as Associate Editor of *America* from 1955 until 1960, when he became Dean of the School of Education at Gonzaga. Since 1962, he has directed Gonzaga-in-Florence as well as the university's honors program. In addition to his many articles and reviews for *America* and other magazines, Father McCluskey's writings include *Public Schools and Moral Education* (1958) and *Catholic Viewpoint on Education* (1959; rev. ed., 1962).